INFINITE GOOD

The Mountains of William James

ALSO BY J. PARKER HUBER

1981
The Wildest Country: Exploring Thoreau's Maine
2008
second revised edition

1999
Elevating Ourselves: Thoreau on Mountains
(editor)

2006
A Wanderer All My Days: John Muir in New England

2010
A Tangle of Asparagus: Letters and Landscapes of My Parents

2012
Living by Loving: Journal of a Solitude at Seventy

2014
Wandering Apart: The Mountains of Henry James

INFINITE GOOD

❧

The Mountains
of William James

J. PARKER HUBER

GREEN WRITERS PRESS   *Brattleboro, Vermont*

Printed in the United States

Green Writers Press is a Vermont-based publisher whose mission is to spread a message of hope and renewal through the words and images we publish. Throughout we will adhere to our commitment to preserving and protecting the natural resources of the earth. To that end, a percentage of our proceeds will be donated to environmental activist groups. Green Writers Press gratefully acknowledges support from individual donors, friends, and readers to help support the environment and our publishing initiative.

GReen
wrITers
press

Giving Voice to Writers Who Will Make the World a Better Place
Green Writers Press | Brattleboro, Vermont
www.greenwriterspress.com

ISBN: 978-0-9961357-9-5

Quotes from *The Correspondence of William James,* edited by Ignas K. Skrupskelis and Elizabeth M. Berkeley, University Press of Virginia (1992-2004), used with permission.

For comments and permission to reprint sections please write:
J. Parker Huber
P.O. Box 360
Brattleboro, Vermont 05302

EDITOR: *Susan Pollack, Gloucester, Massachusetts*
BOOK DESIGN: *Dede Cummings, Brattleboro, Vermont*

COVER: *Mount Chocorua and Chocorua Lake from Tamworth,*
John White Allen Scott, oil on canvas, 1873, 30 x 50
from the collection of John J. and Joan R. Henderson.
Used with permissioin from the Museum of the White Mountains
Plymouth State University, Plymouth, New Hampshire.

TYPESET 12/15 ADOBE CASLON BY DCDESIGN, BRATTLEBORO, VERMONT

PRINTED ON PAPER WITH PULP THAT COMES FROM FSC-CERTIFIED FORESTS, MANAGED FORESTS THAT GUARANTEE RESPONSIBLE ENVIRONMENTAL, SOCIAL, AND ECONOMIC PRACTICES BY LIGHTNING SOURCE. ALL WOOD PRODUCT COMPONENTS USED IN BLACK & WHITE, STANDARD COLOR, OR SELECT COLOR PAPERBACK BOOKS, UTILIZING EITHER CREAM OR WHITE BOOKBLOCK PAPER, THAT ARE MANUFACTURED IN THE LAVERGNE, TENNESSEE PRODUCTION CENTER ARE SUSTAINABLE FORESTRY INITIATIVE® (SFI®) CERTIFIED SOURCING.

In "thankful blessedness" for
Elizabeth Kroll

※

You are the mountain
You are the brook beneath your bed
You are the leaves upon the land
You are the snow entwined in your light brown hair
I am your hand in mine

OCTOBER 2016

There is something in the mountain-air that feeds
the spirit and inspires.

HENRY DAVID THOREAU, *Walking*

✻

I will lift up mine eyes unto the hills, from whence
cometh my help.

Psalm 121, King James Version

Contents

🙵

Part Two

Part Three

INFINITE GOOD

The Mountains of William James

PROLOGUE

🙾

Al Fresco Hours

In May 1860 two teenage brothers, William and Henry James, set forth on a walking excursion. They began their journey in Geneva, Switzerland, traveling (they did not report how) to the hamlet of Chamonix at 3,445 feet in southeast France, at the north base of Mont Blanc (15,771 feet). After a day of rest, they climbed 6,303-foot Montanvert, crossed the Mer de Glace glacier and descended, most likely via the Mauvais Pass. The next day they proceeded mostly on foot for ten hours northeast over the Tête Noire Pass (9,830 feet) to Martigny. Turning south, they made a nine-hour ascent of the Great St. Bernard Pass (8,101 feet), on the Swiss-Italian border, lodging at its famous hospice. Their descent, covering the same ground, consumed another day. By carriage the following day they rode east to Leukerbad (4,629 feet) in the Bernese Oberland.

From there they hiked across the Gemmi Pass (7,599 feet) in seven hours, passing through Kandersteg (3,937 feet), no doubt, before concluding their tour at Interlaken. This was the Jameses' baptism in the Alps, in nature, in the art of saunteringday after day. William would go on to be the mountain climber in the James family, though Henry would do his share of tramping, too. Henry would be the first to return to Switzerland, in 1869. Later, in 1880, 1892 and 1893, William would be there.

What kind of alpinist was William James?
If you survey Maurice Isserman's excellent new history of American mountaineering, you will find Henry David Thoreau and John Muir. In fact, professor Isserman calls Muir, "The greatest figure in American mountaineering, in the nineteenth, or any other century."[2] If you look for William James therein, you will be disappointed, as I was.

According to Muir scholar Terry Gifford, as Muir viewed it, a mountaineer must satisfy four qualifications: He must be a mountain climber, usually invested in reaching the summit; a scientist-naturalist; a person at home in the mountains, and one whose character has been shaped by them.[3] Although James possessed some of these qualities, he did so to a far lesser degree than polestar Muir. James did not make any first ascents; Muir made many. James did not join the leading mountain clubs of his day— Appalachian (AMC,1876), Sierra (1892), and American Alpine (AAC,1902). Muir was a founder of the Sierra Club and served as its first president until his death in 1914. He also was the second president of the AAC, 1908-1910. Yet James did cultivate a special regenerative relationship with mountains.[4]

What makes for mental-moral-spiritual wellness in our culture?

Daily exposure to nature nourished Henry David Thoreau, John Muir, and William James. Immersion in the natural world—sitting, watching, walking; inhaling and exhaling; reading, writing, drawing, painting; horseback riding, bicycling, skating and canoeing; idling—fed them all.

The mountains figured prominently in all three mens' engagement with nature.

Thoreau dwelled in the quiet, pastoral, intimate landscape, surrounding Walden Pond in Concord and Lincoln, Massachusetts. "It is worth the while to see the *Mts* in the horizon once a day," Thoreau believed. From there his blessed Mount Monadnock was visible; he traveled there four times. In 1846, two years after his first ascent of Monadnock, he climbed Maine's Mount Katahdin, almost to its 5,267-foot summit, which, he wrote, gave him more than enough of wilderness: "The tops of mountains are among the unfinished parts of the globe."[5]

"Never while I live will this mountain love die," Muir wrote his wife, Louie, in August 1885. Muir's home was the grand sublime: the sequoias and redwoods, Yosemite Valley and the Sierra Nevada, Alaska and the Grand Canyon. He made long sojourns into the High Sierra including its uppermost Mount Whitney (14,495 feet), in 1873, looking for glaciers and plants. He also ran a successful fruit farm in the Alhambra Valley near Martinez, California, for a decade.[6]

The Adirondacks—where neither Muir nor Thoreau tread—James revealed, had the greatest influence on *his* life. He made annual pilgrimages there in late nineteenth century. He bought land there, as well as a farm at the south base of Mount Chocorua in the White Mountains of New Hampshire, which became his country home. James's singular backpack trip, mostly by horse, not foot, was in Muir's Yosemite and Sierra Nevada in 1898.

William James was not a naturalist like Muir and Thoreau. They along with Darwin were among those inspired by the South American explorations of the great German scientist Alexander von Humboldt (1769-1859). Based in the Andean village of Quito, at 9,350 feet (today in Ecuador), Humboldt climbed "every reachable volcano," from early January to 9 June 1802, according to his recent biographer Andrea Wulf. He ascended Pichincha (15,692 feet), Cotopaxi (19,347 feet), and Antisana (18,714 feet)— despite unfavorable weather, snow, altitude sickness. Humboldt considered Chimborazo, a snowcapped cone reaching 20,577 feet into the sky, "the grandest mountain in the world." (73) Here he attained an altitude of 19,413 feet, which he measured with a barometer, before a snow-filled crevasse curtailed his further ascent. "No one had ever come this high," Wulf stated. "He was the most experienced mountaineer in the world."[7]

I feel a sort of wild joy

James had a naturalist's soul. At age sixteen in March 1858 in Boulogne Sur Mer, France, he wrote his friend Edgar Beach Van Winkle that if he could do what most appealed to him, he'd "get a microscope and go out into the country, into the dear old woods and fields and ponds—there I would try to make as many discoveries as possible." He continued: "When I go out on the beach when I see the sky and the sea and the glorious old cliff I feel a sort of wild joy which makes my hart leap to my throat and the tears come to my eyes." (4:12)

At age twenty-three, James took part in Harvard professor Louis Agassiz's Brazil expedition for ten months, from 29 March 1865 to 29 January 1866. (Agassiz, too, was a protégé of Humboldt.)[8] James's job, while aboard a steamboat, was to help with the collection of specimens of fish, birds, insects along the Amazon River and its tributaries. Though he regarded this as "one of the best spent portions of my life," he concluded, "I thoroughly hate collecting, and long to be back to books. . ." Though he seriously considered a career in nature then, as he had in art earlier, he did not pursue either of these roads. (4:100-134)

After Brazil, the young adventurer returned to Cambridge and to Harvard Medical School, which he had begun in January 1864, before the expedition. After three years of interrupted study James obtained a M.D. in June 1869. He never practiced medicine.

Before joining Agassiz's Brazil venture, even before engaging in his own first walking excursion, with brother Henry in May 1860, William James was attuned to nature. In July 1875, he reflected that he had "first awoke to the rapture of Nature and poetry (some seventeen or eighteen years ago with Browning, Tennyson and Shakspeare's songs) no verse has ever renewed that *feeling* in me as Walt Whitman has succeeded in doing this summer." (4:517) "[S]eventeen or eighteen years ago" would have been 1858 or 1857, when William was fifteen or sixteen, living in France with his family, and mostly studying science, before returning to America in June 1858.

William became increasingly aware of nature's beneficence. In 1872, then thirty, he confided to Henry in two letters what he had drawn from his Maine coast experiences that summer. In the first, of 24 August, he wrote that the "nervouspuckers" of his mind had been "smoothed out gently & fairly by the sweet influences of many a lie on a hill top at mt. Desert with sky & sea & Islands before me, by many a row, and a couple of sails, and by my bath and siesta on the blazing sand this morn." (1:165) And, again in the fall of 1872, he wrote that he had "never so much as this summer felt the soothing and hygienic effects of nature upon the human spirit." Earlier his enjoyment of nature had been a "luxury, but this time t'was as a vital food, or medicine." (1:173) And so it remained for his life.

> The holidays of life are its most vitally significant portions, just because they are, or at least should be, covered with this kind of magically irresponsible spell.
> "On a Certain Blindness," (162)

William James needed "two solid months of loafing to go through the year of work," he wrote Philosophy Professor George Holmes Howison from Keene Valley, New York, on 6 August 1883. (5:567) For James leisure was a path to nature. Both were required: nature and leisure. One abetted the other. He advocated for both. Drawing on exemplary naturalists and poets, James made a cogent case for idleness.[9]

In April 1899, when *Talks to Teachers* was published, James sent a copy to Pauline Goldmark, his climbing companion and friend, desiring her to read his essay "On a Certain Blindness." (8:517) In this essay, James revealed that our observation of an individual may not convey the whole truth of him or her, forwhat may appear "vacant" behavior to the observer may bestow great gifts upon the observed. Wordsworth, for example, felt an ineffable delight in "tramping the hills" of the Lake District. It was estimated that he walked 180,000 miles. James imagined that Wordsworth's "rural neighbors, tightly and narrowly intent upon their own affairs, their crops and lambs and fences, must have thought him a very insignificant and foolish personage." Yet for the poet these rambles in nature were a source of exuberant creativity and joy. So on walked Wordsworth in "thankful blessedness." (153-154)[10]

Whitman "felt the human crowd as rapturously as Wordsworth felt the mountains," according to James. As proof, he offered Whitman's "Crossing Brooklyn Ferry," calling it "a divinely beautiful poem." (155-156)

Another kindred spirit included in James's essay was the English naturalist Richard Jefferies. From his *The Story of My Heart* (1883), James absorbed how his "intense communion . . . held with the earth, the sun and sky," filled him with rapture and ecstasy. (154) Jefferies walked every day, discovering "A fullness of physical life causes a deeper desire of soul-life."[11]

Another English naturalist James admired was William Henry Hudson. Born in Argentina to American parents, Hudson came to London in 1874 at age thirty-three. From Hudson's memoir of his Argentine youth, *Idle Days in Patagonia* (1893), James took note of Hudson's daily ritual of "noonday pause," wherein he returned to the same spot to sit still for an hour. "My state was one of *suspense* and *watchfulness*," Hudson remarked. His mind was suspended, as in meditation, and the world was absorbed through his senses. (161-162) (I, too, experience such moments when bicycling all days hither and yon, all weathers, embracing the elements, grateful to be unconfined by house or car.) Thoreau espoused a similar way of wandering in his essay "Walking," which celebrates "Wildness,"[12] He wrote: "When a traveller asked Wordsworth's servant to show him her master's study, she answered, 'Here is his library, but his study is out of doors.'"

Then, too, Thoreau himself sauntered away his afternoons in woods and wetlands. The dweller at Walden wrote: "There were times when I could not afford to sacrifice the bloom of the present moment to any work, whether of the head or hands. I love a broad margin to my life." He observed, "This was sheer idleness to my fellow-townsmen, no doubt . . . A man must find his occasions in himself."[13]

We want to be aware of what other persons are experiencing, not impose our beliefs, our values on them based on outer appearances. Thoreau, Wordsworth, and James would all have agreed on this.

James wanted us to hold a "higher vision of an inner significance." He concluded that such an experience does not depend on the occasion, but on the soul. "It all depends on the capacity of the soul to be grasped, to have its life-currents absorbed by what is given." (159)

James needed mountains. To free himself of mind-thinking. To become body-moving, feet-boots-tramping on earth, solid rock, rugged roots, moist mud. To be Thoreau on Katahdin coming in contact with nature and feeling "the presence of a force not bound to be kind to man."[14] To rest his mind in exertion, in scenery, in mystery, in nothing.

The mountains kept James alive. They bestowed

blessings upon him. Foremost was recreation: recreation in its deeper meaning of re-creating oneself. Next, restoration of health and well-being. "What I *need* is to regain nervous *tone*, which brings health of soul with it, and that is what the blessed mountains and a moderate amount of solitude for a time can give," he wrote his wife Alice from Brig, Switzerland, on 1 August 1892. (7:307)

We see again and again how mountains restored James's soul, rejuvenated his body and mind. He repeatedly praised their benefits. His nerves calmed. Even their presence fed his spirit and made him whole again. "The 10 days of mountaineering did me worlds of good." James wrote brother Henry from Switzerland on 24 August 1892. "A man comes near to 'finding his true self' in the condition into which these tramps put him, even if they be as insignificant as the 6 hour excursions which we took." (2:226-227)

So, too, biologist and *Silent Spring* author Rachel Carson found this positive connection in nature. "Her words, and her life, teach that a close relationship with the natural world is a source of strength, healing, and renewal," according to Philosophy Professor Kathleen Dean Moore.[15]

And yet, as we shall see, a momentous event occurred. William James's over-exertion in his beloved Adirondacks caused him a heart injury that all but ended his climbing days. These peaks were known to him. Though, as any mountain climber can tell you, the known can become unknown in the blink of an eye. No two ascents are the same. Everything changes. Risks abound. I recall arriving atop tranquil Mount Monadnock (3,165 feet) in southwest New Hampshire on the first day of spring, euphoric. Minutes later I was stunned. A thick fog swept away familiarity. The cairns and white paint marking the trails disappeared. Blindly, I scrambled this way and that searching for the descent. Eventually, I had to give up the hope of finding the same way I had come up on, and settled for the one that was visible to me, even though it lead in another direction.

The Traveler

Herein you will also see, William James as traveler, especially in the summers bookended by Harvard's academic year. His father, Henry James Sr (1811-1882) was an international traveler enabled by his father, William James (1771-1832) of Albany, New York, who was "one of the richest and most powerful men in the nation."[16] His generosity left Henry Sr "leisured for life." This income, largely from Syracuse, New York, properties, assured independence for Henry James Sr to travel and for his family.

As a youth Henry James Sr had hunted and fished, walked in the woods, but he did not climb mountains, biographer Habegger relates. At age thirteen in 1824, tragedy struck. Attempting to quell a fire caused by a fireball from a hot-air balloon alighting in an Albany stable, he burned his leg so severely that he had to endure two surgeries to remove it and four years of convalescence.[17]

This did not prevent Henry Sr from traveling, to provide the best education for his children. The family moved about a lot when William, the eldest child, was growing up; this locomotion became familiar, and would shape William's life. Shortly after he was born in Astor House, in New York City, in January 1842, the James family moved to 5 Washington Square, where on 15 April 1843, Henry Jr was born. In October 1843, the James family sailed to England, later traveling to France before returning to New York, in 1845, where, on 21 July, brother Garth Wilkinson (Wilky) was born. The family steamed up the Hudson River to Albany, where brother Robertson was born, on 29 August 1846. During the 1840s and 1850s, Albany became a second home to the Jameses. In New York, the family moved into their own brownstone at 58 West 14th Street, in time for sister Alice's arrival, on 7 August 1848. The Jameses lived abroad again from July 1855 to June 1858. Returning to the States, they settled in Newport, Rhode Island. After another year abroad (1859-1860), the family moved back to Newport, then to Boston, and finally, in 1866, to Cambridge, Massachusetts (20 Quincy Street), where the elder Jameses lived for the rest of their lives.[18]

Change, William James concluded later in life, is "perhaps the most imperative of human needs." (11:228) It certainly was for him; he explained: "change of scenery and life is a vital necessity without which I go out like a fire that isn't poked. I regret it, for if there is anything I *aspire* to, it is to be able to work steadily on day after day with no need of change, but my bad nervous temperament keeps me exiled from that Eden." (8:74)

William James was aware of his own deep, inner need for change, even as he longed for constancy. He embraced this contradiction. A generation earlier, naturalist George Perkins Marsh pondered this paradox in his 1864 book *Man and Nature*. Addressing what we can do to restore the health of the planet, Marsh said it was critical to be mindful of motion, of our "incessant fluctuation." He observed, "It is time for some abatement in the restless love of change which characterizes us." Marsh's call for "this settling down," says Professor Emeritus John Elder, "could foster a greater capacity for attention to the natural world and a deeper affiliation with our surroundings."[19]

Surely James needed both traveling and staying put. He struggled to balance them, to maintain equilibrium. In Cambridge he walked from his Irving Street home along Kirkland Street to the college chapel for a fifteen-minute service before nine o'clock. He walked home for lunch and took an obligatory nap before returning to campus. After work he might bicycle about, stroll to visit friends, and, in winter, skate on Fresh Pond (8:5, 5 January 1895)

By contrast, Thoreau, while he lived at home, excelled in solo sauntering: slow, silent local locomotion. He walked about, visiting his plant friends. That is not to say he did not board a train for Maine, Montreal, Minnesota. The essential Thoreau was content to be in place to satisfy his curiosity and writing with what was near, within walking, boating distance. Thoreau thrived on the abundance around him that stimulated the "greater abundance within."[20]

This book is an attempt, by no means definitive, to reveal the significant role that mountains played in sustaining the remarkable life of William James. The mountains were part of him and he of them. Let us now join William James, aged forty-three, in the fullness of his life, as he departs Cambridge, in June 1895.

PART ONE

In Sight of Monadnock, 1895

On Sunday 9 June 1895, William James and his wife, Alice, boarded the train for Vermont to visit the Kiplings. Harvard's spring term had just ended, liberating Professor James to wander where he would. Because Cambridge summers offered the philosopher "pure fag with no refreshment," he presided elsewhere as much as possible. (2:213)

Three and a half years earlier, on 18 January 1892, James's brother Henry, the writer, had given away Caroline Balestier in marriage to Rudyard Kipling—both twenty-six—at All Souls Church, Langham Place, London. "[A] dreary little wedding," Henry had written William, "with an attendance simply of 4 men—her mother & sister prostrate with influenza." (2:199n7, 200) Henry signed their marriage certificate as witness, which remained in a Brattleboro, Vermont, bank until discovered in 1991. Despite Henry's lack of faith in the union's future, it lasted until Rudyard's death in 1936.[1]

The month before the wedding, Henry James had attended the funeral of the bride's brother Charles Wolcott Balestier, a writer and literary publisher, who "had taken a drink of contaminated water," and died of virulent typhoid in Dresden, Germany, according to literary critic and biographer Leon Edel. Thereafter, James wrote Wolcott's mother, Anna Smith Balestier, on each anniversary of Wolcott's death.[2]

On 4 February 1892, Henry bade farewell to the newlyweds as they boarded the *Teutonic* at Liverpool to begin a planned trip around the world. He also introduced them to another passenger, the historian Henry Adams, whose autobiography would gratefully recall Kipling as an "exuberant fountain of gaiety and wit."[3] (2:200-201)

Upon arrival in New York, the Kiplings entrained for Brattleboro, arriving at midnight on 17 February 1892. Caroline's younger brother, Beatty Balestier, met them at the depot. Bundled in blankets and buffalo robes, in an open sleigh, with horses' bells jingling, they traveled over the moonlit snow to Beatty's home.

In the summer of 1895, William and Alice James would travel these same four miles. It is likely that the Kiplings had despatched their English coachman, Matthew Howard, in their new phaeton with a pair of horses to fetch the Jameses at the station in the heart of Brattleboro, then a village of six-thousand souls. (Neither of the Kiplings drove.) At the time, the five-story Brooks House (guests) and the steepled Baptist Church dominated the west side of Main Street. Between them, on the northwest corner of Main and High streets in the early 1820s, Jonathan Hunt had built a handsome two-and-one-half-story Federal to accommodate his wife, Jane Maria, and their five children to-be. Here, embowered in elms, on 31 March 1824, William Morris Hunt was born.

Did William James connect the place and the person? In the fall of 1858 and winter of 1861, in Newport, Rhode Island, William Morris Hunt was his art teacher. During the latter Newport period, Henry James and artist John La Farge had joined William as Hunt's pupils. All three had encouraged William James's talent. William Hunt's younger brother, Richard Morris Hunt, (also born in Brattleboro, on 31 October 1827), designed many of Newport's mansions.

The Hunt family's Vermont residency did not last long. William and Richard's father, attorney Jonathan Hunt, elected to the U.S. House of Representatives in 1827, thereafter spent much of his time in Washington; his wife, Jane, and family joined him there in November 1830. During Jonathan's third term, on 15 May 1832, he died of cholera. Temporarily Jane Hunt returned to Brattleboro before resettling the family in New Haven, Connecticut, in October 1832.

Living at the old Hunt house when William and Alice James rode by were Colonel George White Hooker and his wife, Minna G. Fisk. Hooker was partners with Corser & Mitchell in the manufacturing of overalls on Flat Street.[4]

Proceeding northward on Main Street to the common, the Jameses likely would have noticed construction: Rails were being laid in the road for the trolley, a form of transportation familiar to them from Cambridge. (The Cambridge line had been electrified in 1889.) Two blocks north of the Hunt house, the new track encroached a bit too closely upon Wells Fountain (William Rutherford

Mead's 1890 design). This made it difficult for horses to be watered, so the track had to be moved.

Undoubtedly later, the Jameses learned of Kipling's distaste for the trolley. In a letter, Kipling argued on aesthetic grounds, it "wholly destroys the beauty for which Brattleboro is so justly famous," and he raised safety issues: it "increases the risk of fires" and "accident from direct collision with the cars," humans and horses.[5]

In another block, the landscape opened onto the common, on the west side of the road, and onto the Richards Bradley farm on the east; the farm's main house still stands, now converted to a residential care home. Then the Jameses crossed the covered bridge over the West River, where it meets the Connecticut River. The Abenaki called the West River Wantastiquet, meaning "head or source of the river." The name is retained in Mount Wantastiquet (1,351 feet) which accompanied the Jameses from the depot along the Connecticut River's New Hampshire shore, and would for another mile.[6]

At Waite Farm—which in another two months would serve as the Kiplings' private post office, with Anna Waite handling their mail—William and Alice James turned left onto Black Mountain Road, which in three miles reached that eminence, of 1,280 feet "sculpted by glacial ice," and distinguished as "the only granite bald in the southern half of the state," according to ecologist Tom Wessels. Black Mountain is also "the only place in Vermont where bear oak grows," Wessels observes. The tree's acorns feed the bears. The mountain also supports a hundred acres of red pines, and the very rare three birds orchid, now preserved by the Nature Conservancy.[7]

The Jameses continued uphill along Waite Brook on its way south from Rice Farm to the Connecticut River. Just over the Brattleboro-Dummerston town line, they turned left into the drive that inclined to the Kipling house, which they entered from the far side.

In addition to the Jameses, joining the Kiplings' customary afternoon tea were architect Henry Rutgers Marshall of New York and writer Mary R. Cabot of Brattleboro. Marshall, a friend of the Jameses and a student of the late architect Henry Hobson Richardson (1838-1886), had designed the Kipling home. It was named Naulakha (precious jewel) after the Kipling-Wolcott novel. Evident here is Richardson's signature Shingle Style. A ninety-by-thirty-foot dwelling on an above-ground, native-mortared-stone foundation, Naulakha sits in a meadow on the side of a hill that rises over 700 feet, its long sides facing east and west. A plazza along the short end of the house ends in a garden running southward.[8]

Sitting on the piazza that beautiful Sunday, the Kiplings and their guests sipped tea and looked east across farm and forest of the Connecticut River valley to the New Hampshire hills. Thirty miles distant Mount Monadnock appeared "a gigantic thumbnail pointing heavenward"—as Rudyard had described it in one of his American travel letters, "In Sight of Monadnock," dated 18 February 1892. Emerson's long poem "Monadnoc," had touched Kipling when he was a schoolboy. "Monadnock came to mean everything that was helpful, healing, and full of quiet, and when I saw him half across New Hampshire he did not fail," wrote the poet and story-teller from India. This view had clinched for the Kiplings the site of their home. They bought eleven and a half acres.[9]

The Kiplings were part of a "large farming community." Southward across the road from Naulakha, Mother Balestier lived at Beechwood and contiguous, to her north, resided Caroline's brother, Beatty, with wife and infant at Maplewood. Today Beechwood and Naulakha still grace what is now Kipling Road (though still dirt). Maplewood, destroyed by fire in 1904, has been replaced by another farmhouse, though the original barn remains. Five other residences now occupy the third of a mile between Beechwood and the former Maplewood site.[10]

The Kiplings and the William Jameses had met before. In December 1894, Rudyard and Carrie had traveled to Cambridge. The Kiplings stayed with Susan and Charles Eliot Norton, at their Shady Hill estate—where Rudyard had visited in September 1893 (while Carrie stayed with baby Josephine, born 29 December 1892)—but they enjoyed the nearby James family. Daughter Peggie James's home-made peanut candy made them "sticky and inarticulate," Rudyard wrote Henry James. "It all seemed delightfully intimate and friendly."[11]

In the spring of 1895, the Kiplings had traveled to Washington, DC (6 March-6 April 1895), where they conversed with Henry Adams, John Hay, TheodoreRoosevelt (7 March; since 1889 Civil Service Commissioner; soon to be New York City Police Commissioner) and President Grover Cleveland at the White House (5 April).[12]

the purring of the warm, happy world

Returning home the Kiplings observed spring's advent. Eagerly, they tended their garden and trees. In mid-April, Rudyard reported their first wildflower, "a liver-wort" and that "the new maple sugar has been made."[13] Named for its leaf shape, liverwort or liverleaf or hepatica (Greek for liver) is among Vermont's first spring beauties; it is especially lush at Esther Falks's off Bunker Road, three-and-a-half miles north of Naulakha. In early June, the Kiplings and Jameses witnessed the last of spring's spell of enchantment: deciduous trees rinsed in fresh pale greens, mixed with the deeper green spikes of pine and hemlock.

Kipling called spring the "Time of New Talk" in his story "The Spring Running," from *The Second Jungle Book*, with which he entertained the Jameses. The story concerns the last adventure of Mowgli, the seventeen-year-old Master of the Jungle. The Indian spring, like no other anywhere, sounded like "the purring of the warm, happy world," Kipling wrote. Even though not feeling well, Mowgli went north: sometimes by "ground-going," sometimes by "tree road." This time, however, this vernal exercise did not renew him. That took the powers of Messua, his mother, who thought him "beautiful beyond all men." She gave warmmilk for his fever. Sleeping all night, the next day he rose restored, able to return.[14]

Kipling also shared with his guests "The Song of the Banjo," its having just arrived within June's *New Review*, an English magazine. What James made of this sixteen stanza ballad with various refrains of the banjo player's "Tunka-tunka-tunka-tunka-tunk" is not recorded.[15]

Did Kipling ever climb Monadnock? Was he an alpinist? John Walker, Honorary Librarian of the Kipling Society in Ashford, Kent, England, kindly responded to my inquiry: "He wrote well—even convincingly, of Monadnock, the Khyber pass, the Green Mountains, and the Rockies (he called them 'the not so Little Brothers of the Himalayas') but I can find no evidence of him doing any real climbing. He seems never to have actually visited Monadnock.

When he wrote of 'old bald mountains that have parted with every shred of verdure, and stand wrapped in sheets of wrinkled silver rock' he is observing from a train!"[16]

Kipling did make a "one day-long excursion up the flanks of Wantastiquet," their "guardian mountain," he related in his autobiography, *Something of Myself*.[17] Did he know of Thoreau's ascent of the same alp of 9 September 1856?

Leaving Naulaka, Alice James returned to Cambridge, while William headed west, stopping in Willliamstown, Massachusetts, to visit Professor John Edward Russell for twenty-four hours. He continued on to Albany (3:30 P.M. on Tuesday 11 June), Amsterdam, Utica, and Syracuse, New York. William and Alice kept in touch via the mail. On 16 June 1895 from Springfield Center, New York, William wrote Henry of their visit to the Kiplings: "[W]e combined very well together for 36 hours." (2:364)

After the Jameses departed, so did the Kiplings. On 1 July they brought Josephine to stay with Mrs. Balestier at the Fairview Inn in East Gloucester, Massachusetts; then they sailed for England, not returning to Brattleboro until 22 August.

In mid-September the Kiplings took the train north to Newbury, New Hampshire, at the southern end of Lake Sunapee. From there they followed the east shore, probably by carriage, 2.2 miles north to the Fells, the summer home of John and Clara Hay. Built in 1891-1892 the Fells offers a commanding view of the seven-and-a-half-mile-long lake, an "ice-gashed bedrock basin," and of Mount Sunapee (2,743 feet) at its southern end.[18]

Near the end of the following summer of 1896, the Kiplings's situation changed dramatically. A feud with

Carrie's cantankerous brother, Beatty, forced the Kiplings to leave Naulakha on 29 August 1896 and America on 1 September—a little after three years there—never to return.[19]

AS PRETTY AS EYE COULD WISH

🙰

Southwest New Hampshire, Summers 1885 & 1886

Alice and William knew intimately the Grand Monadnock (3,165 feet) before viewing it with the Kiplings, from Naulakha, for, a decade earlier, the Jameses had summered in the foothills of Monadnock.

In mid-June 1885, William had arrived in the Monadnock region of southwest New Hampshire to search for summer lodgings. Accompanying him were sons Harry, six, and William, three, and Alice's sister Margaret, who assisted with child care. They stayed at "an elevated farm, near West Harrisville Station, five miles from" the Appleton House in Dublin, from which William wrote Alice on 19 June. "The P.O is Pottersville." (6:34, 41) In this hamlet of southwest Harrisville in the late eighteenth and early nineteenth centuries artisans had turned the superb clay into reputable domestic wares.

James found suitable lodgings for the whole family on the farm of Frederick J. Lawrence (1851-1929), who with his wife, Clara, took in boarders. (7:91n3) The place—now a private residence—is tucked away in an intervale in the town of Jaffrey, between Thorndike and Frost ponds, below Woodbury Hill (1,359 feet) to the northwest. Two miles south is the trig village of Jaffrey Center, which offered summer travelers the Monadnock Inn (c.1850), which began accepting guests in1870 and still continues.[1] The Jameses rented three rooms for a total of $22 aweek, which included the services of a maid. The family spent two summers there. (As a full professor at Harvard since 1884, James earned $500 a year.) William extolled the virtues of their "exceptionally blissful" vacation to sister Alice: "the table first rate, the people angels, the country roundabout as pretty as eye could wish." (6:65, 155)

Monadnock, whose summit lay three-and-a-half miles west, watched over them. At the time the surrounding landscape and the mountain itself were largely cleared for pasture. Today (11 August 2011) one can no longer see the mountain from the Lawrence farmhouse. Tall trees obscure it. James may have climbed Monadnock several times, though his correspondence only mentions one ascent. Then again, the various ailments he suffered may have limited his activities, as they would later. In September 1885, for example, while at Putnam Camp in Keene Valley in the Adirondacks, William did not undertake any "big walks and climbs." (6: 71n2, 79,151)

Though Monadnock can be climbed from all four directions, the most popular ascent was then from the south. This was due to Mountain House, which could accommodate a hundred guests and was accessed from the Troy-Jaffrey road by a straight one-mile-plus carriage road. From there the White Arrow Trail, believed to be the mountain's oldest, rose a mile to the summit. Likely James went this way.

A new trail, laid out in 1884, however, provided another option for James. It began at the southeast corner of Dublin Lake, four miles directly northwest of the Lawrence farm. It was called the Pumpelly after its creator, Raphael Pumpelly, "a great blue-eyed giant with a long flowing beard, a vivacious tongue, and a courtly manner." Pumpelly, his wife, Eliza Frances Shepard, and their four children had recently moved into a grand new shingle style house, Auf de Höhe (On the Heights), on Snow Hill, above Dublin Lake's east end. (Prior to this, they had summered in Newport, Rhode Island, where they had built a home in 1881 on Gibbs Avenue. But they had found Newport's climate too enervating.) Pumpelly's namesake path, running four-and-a-half miles from lake to summit, gave the family ready entrance to elysium.[2]

It appears that the Jameses and the Pumpellys did not meet during the summers of 1885 and 1886. Pumpelly was busy elsewhere. On 18 July 1885, Pumpelly, then forty-seven, left Dublin Lake in a horse-drawn wagon with driver for northwestern Massachusetts, where he led a team of men in a geologic survey of the Green Mountains. He would continue that work for the next several summers, through 1888, finally submitting his *Geology of the Green Mountains* to John Wesley Powell, head of the U.S. Geological Survey in Washington, DC, on 18 January 1892.[3]

Undoubtedly, however, James and Pumpelly knew each other. They both lived in Cambridge; they both were Harvard professors. After marrying on 20 October 1869, Pumpelly and Eliza settled at 10 Trowbridge Street, where former-slave Harriet Jacobs had boarded Harvard faculty and students. Pumpelly accepted Josiah Whitney's offer to be the first professor of mining in Harvard's new department of geology, of which Whitney was head. That fall of 1869 William informed Henry of Pumpelly's forthcoming book, *Across America and Asia: Notes of a Five Years' Journey around the World* (1870), in which William's art teacher, John La Farge, wrote "An Essay on Japanese Art." (1:101,103n4,129) In 1883, Pumpelly had been elected to the Saturday Club that met monthly in Boston's Parker House, perhaps sometimes with William James present, as James had been a member since 1881.[4]

Pursuing the Northern Transcontinental Survey in 1882 and 1883, Pumpelly discovered the first glacier in what is now Glacier National Park (1910) in Montana— the first "by a professional geologist," his biographer qualified. Named for him, this glacier sits atop Blackfoot Mountain (9,574 feet) along the Continental Divide, south of Gunsight Pass.

Like all glaciers in the park, it is now sadly diminished. On the day I wrote this (18 June 2010), I opened the July/ August issue of *Sierra* and found on page 19: "Glacier National Park loses two more glaciers." Startled, I inquired of their names, but could not find out.[5]

———

Most summers it was difficult for William James to stay put for long. There were invitations to visit friends and a deep desire to be elsewhere than Cambridge. James thought it wise to retain the "freedom to travel." (6:155) "This knocking about is a splendid thing for me," he expressed to Alice. (6:162) Then again, as he wrote a friend, he wished he "could live in the country all the year round, or rather 9 months of it," (6:164) T. S. Eliot framed the paradox in *Four Quartets*: "We must be still and still moving."

So while enjoying Monadnock in August 1886, William and Alice left their children there to visit their Boston friend, Mary Gray Ward Dorr (Molly), at her summer home, Oldfarm, in Bar Harbor on Mount Desert Island, Maine. Also there was Molly's thirty-three-year-old, bachelor son. George Bucknam Dorr, renowned for his devotion to Mount Desert's wildness. On 12 August 1901, at the urging of Harvard's president Charles W. Eliot, a longtime summer resident of Mount Desert's Northeast Harbor, George Dorr met with him and others to form a corporation to preserve the island. Their efforts culminated in the designation of Mount Desert as a national monument in 1916, and as a national park three years later. "[F] ever attacks" kept William abed, he wrote Henry, for eight of their twelve days there. They returned to Cambridge on 23 August for two nights before going back to Jaffrey and the children.[6] (2:46, 6:574)

In early September 1886, William returned Down East. Off Kittery Point, he surveyed land on Gerrish Island, but concluded it was not suitable for a summer residence. (6:148) Then he took "a little trip" north to the White Mountains. (2:51) On 5-6 September, he inspected a farm of 75 acres—a third in hay and the rest in oak and pine— with a "little house & large barn" for sale in Chocorua and in view of the eponymous lake and mountain. A second look at it on 11 September decided him in its favor. (6:159-162, 164) The next day he returned to Jaffrey, then home to Cambridge on the 25th, where he told his sister of his vacation, "I never spent a better one myself." (6:167) Purchase of the Chocorua property was made in November. (2:51-52) The Jameses' desire to own a country home and to spend the summer elsewhere than Cambridge was met.

———

Not until September 1905 did William James himself return to the Monadnock region. The draw was his old friend Thomas Perry, who with his wife, Lilla Cabot, and family lived in Hancock, New Hampshire, on the northeast side of the mountain. This time James came alone, stayed a weekend and climbed another mountain.

In the summer of 1907 William and Alice James's son Alexander (born 22 December 1890) would come to visit the artist Abbott Handerson Thayer and family at their home on the south side of Dublin Lake. Inspired by Thayer, Alexander would become an artist, studying under Thayer's guidance. In 1919 Aleck and his wife, Frederika Paine (wed in 1916), moved to Dublin, where, except for one intersession in France in 1929-1930, they remained for life. In 1920 they built a home on Old County Road in the lower village of Dublin, to which a studio was added in 1944, just before Aleck's death on 26 February 1946. Both buildings still remain in private hands.[7]

AT THE PORTALS OF THAT
ADIRONDACK WILDERNESS

※

16 *June 1895*

After leaving the Kiplings, William James paused in his travels. He stayed at a farm called Swanswick, near Springfield Center, New York, at the north end of seven-mile-long Otsego Lake, where he'd taken an early morning swim. (8:568) On Sunday, 16 June 1895, he wrote Alice: "Swanswick is a perfect paradise." (8:39) In another letter, to artist Sarah Wyman Whitman, James confided, "[A]t the portals of that Adirondack wilderness for the breath of which I have sighed for years." He added: "just about to get a little health into me." He hungered for "the smell of the spruce, the feel of the moss, the sound of the cataract, the bath in its waters, the divine outlook from the cliff or hill top over the unbroken forest." He wished that she also "aspired to the wilderness." (8:41) The next day James set out for the Adirondacks, taking the railroad from Utica (28 miles northwest of Otsego) to Lake Placid, "inquisitive as to the scenery along that new line." (8:39) *two delicious days*

When, on the night of 18 June, James arrived at the Adirondack Lodge, it was closed.

The lodge stood about eight miles south from the Lake Placid station. However, innkeeper Henry Van Hoevenberg, whom he met for the first time, made him welcome. Hoevenberg, called Mr. Van, was younger than James, forty-six to fifty-three years, and shorter, five-feet three inches to five-feet, eight. Both trim and nimble. In 1877 atop Mount Marcy, Van and his fiancée, Josephine Scofield, had chosen Clear Lake for their home. She, however, did not live to return with him the next summer. Nonetheless, he went ahead and purchased 640 acres and began construction of the grand three-story, spruce-log structure with a seven-story observation tower, which opened for guests in the summer of 1880. When he met James, Van had been innkeeper, raconteur, guide, trail maker and mender for fifteen years. He laid out the shortest trail to Marcy, named for him as is nearby Mount Hoevenberg (2,860 feet)[1]. That same year, 1895, Van had had to give up the inn to meet the expenses of litigation over his telegraph patents.

Here James spent "two delicious days," though rainy, alone, reading. Then on the 21st he went to Thomas Davidson's on East Hill, outside of Keene Valley, where he proposed climbing Hurricane Mountain before going to Chocorua. (8:46, 568)

COLORADO HAS NOW BECOME
A PART OF MY SELF

※

August 1895: *Colorado*

Cheyenne Mountain (9,565 feet), Pikes Peak (14,110 feet)

Before James left the East Coast, he drew sustenance from a July fortnight at Chocorua, which was filled with plenty of physical exercise. Atop Mount Chocorua (3,500 feet), he parted from daughter Peggy and son Henry and made a brisk descent, reaching home, a distance of five miles, in two hours instead of the normal three hours. Then he traveled by train to Cambridge to begin a month of summer school teaching at Norwich Free Academy in Norwich, Connecticut, (15-17 July) and at Harvard (18-29 July) and then onto Colorado. (8:55, 56n1; 569)

"*Here*, it is delicious," James wrote his "Beloved wife" upon his arrival in Colorado Springs (6,008 feet) on 1 August 1895. After three days and nights of rail travel,

James was relieved to step again onto terra firma and inhale Colorado's dry, bracing air and inhabit a landscape completely new to him. (2:372; 8:59)

Five days later he gave brother Henry this picture of his place. "Five thousand feet above the sea, & the illimitable prairie diversified by low bluffs, and shaded with the most exquisite tints of blue green and gray reaching to the eastward horizon, whilst on the west the Rocky mountains, only a couple of miles off, rise abruptly up, as if breathed on a canvass scene in their exquisite pink delicacy of modulation, and form a magnificent background. It is now the rainy season, and everything is green. But the storms keep in the mountains, which every afternoon fill themselves with the most glorious rain and cloud and lightning-effects." (2:372) In "the most glorious rain" we hear John Muir's voice.

This was James's first trip west of the Hundredth Meridian. He had come to give six lectures to teachers at the Colorado Summer School of Science, Philosophy, and Languages at Colorado College.

His Colorado Springs hostess, Elizabeth Cass Goddard, "came here for her son's health and lost him a couple of years ago," William wrote home. She was "angelic" and "greatly beloved in the community" of 11,040 souls (1890 census). "My conditions in this charming house are perfect," Alice learned (8:60). 808 North Cascade Avenue, like Kipling's Naulakha, was a creation of architect Henry Rutgers Marshall. Marshall also designed the First Congregational Church (1887-1888)—three blocks south of the Goddard residence—at 20 East Saint Vrain Street on the corner with Tejon—a building which did not appeal to James. Was its Romanesque style not to his taste? Its size, scale too grand for him, like the city of London's? (3:64) Its multi-pillared portico too cavernous? Its proportions not simple and true, as Thoreau would have wished. Surely, however, James must have approved of its earthy exterior of rhyolite from nearby Castle Rock.[1]

Coincidentally, James was now enjoying Marshall's new little book, *Aesthetic Principles*. To Marshall, aesthetics was "the science of what gives pleasure, whether by beauty . . . or by mere novelty, vividness, or richness of suggestion," James wrote in his review. "[T]his theory, like all aesthetic theories, sounds so *skinny* in comparison with the richness of the phenomena it includes that one wonders how principles so trivial should account for results so significant and precious." This reading was timely as James opened to the majestically beautiful Colorado mountains.[2] (8:84, 571-572)

"Pure excursions and social engagements" occupied James. He was not even able to write his wife everyday. On 4 August, he reached the 14,111-foot-summit of Pikes Peak "by the ignominious method of a cog railroad," believing this mode of locomotion preferable to the "12 hours or more on foot." According to the then new Baedeker of *The United States* (1893), the train took about two hours to rise 7,500 feet, a distance of 8.75 miles, to the top. A seventeen-mile carriage road and a bridle path were other options. "The scenery on the way up was wonderfully fine," James related, "but the top view was disappointing from its too great extent." (8:60-61) Pikes Peak was his lifetime's highest mountain elevation.

The next day Leigh Wentworth Chamberlin (1869-1904) took him on a twenty-mile drive around the foothills, and through the Garden of the Gods with its red sandstone sculptures.

On 7 August, James ascended Cheyenne Mountain (9,565 feet), eleven miles southwest of Colorado Springs. "A glorious day," he wrote Alice, "and a very nice easy walk, rather less than going up Chocorua." If he had started from Old Stage Road his ascent would have been a thousand feet, in two-and-a half miles, as compared to Chocorua's elevation gain of 3,000 feet, from his home, in five miles. What a difference the dry air made to the unperspiring James, while aspiring upward. (8:65)

After his last lecture on Friday 9 August, James's desire to tour "this magnificent country" further trumped his desire to go home. Besides he had "a free pass over some of the finest scenery in the mountains accessible by rail." (8:67)

He spent an initial night in a "first rate little hotel" over 7,000 feet in Salida. In 1880 the railroad created this small town of 2,586 people—first called South Arkansas after the river that flowed through it. The Monte Cristo at the station and the St. Clair west of the river offered lodgings. James does not name his hotel. Let's say he slept at the closer one. To the south he would have taken in the northern peaks of the Sangre de Cristos and to the north the Collegiate Peaks, the highest of which is Harvard at 14,420 feet, named in 1869 by Harvard's geology professor, Josiah Dwight Whitney.

———

Since 1997 Salida has been home to one of Colorado's leading writers Susan J. Tweit and, until his death in 2011, her husband, Richard Cabe, "an abstract sculptor who works in found boulders, steel, and wood," as Tweit described him in her memoir. A few blocks from the post office, the couple built a house. They restored a derelict duplex for his shop, while also restoring the land with native grasses and wildflowers. And they planted a kitchen garden which fed them for ten months of the year. They created a gravel court for Richard's favorite game of French bowling, pelanque. Since settling in Salida, Tweit has written a weekly newspaper column for *The Salida Mountain Mail*, essays for *Audubon*, *National Parks* and others, and books, most recently *Colorado's Scenic Byways* (2008), *Colorado Less Traveled* (2005), *The San Luis Valley* (2005). Year round the beauty of their home, land and the surrounding mountains nourished their souls. Her daily haikus appear on Twitter and Facebook.[3]

Back to James's journey: On 13 August he rose at dawn to catch the train. A day of "first class scenery" over Marshall Pass (10,846 feet) of the Sawatch Range of the Rockies, containing Colorado's highest mountain, Elbert (14,433), and along the Gunnison River through Black Canyon to Grand Junction (4,580 feet), covering 208 miles by six P.M.[4] This was the farthest west that James traveled on this trip.

When in 1890 Rudyard Kipling crossed the United States, west to east, his train came through the Black Canyon of the Gunnison, although from the opposite direction. Kipling remembered: it was a "mad ride which

I felt keenly . . . until I had to stop to offer prayers for the safety of the train."[5]

———

Meanwhile, after reaching Grand Junction, James's train turned eastward towards the Atlantic. Three more train hours over eighty-nine miles brought James to Glenwood Springs (5,746 feet) at the junction of Roaring Fork and Grand River. The Colorado "hotel is really superb—handsome and *simple*—it makes one expand to be in it," he wrote Alice the next morning. Then he reflected on his experience: "it is a waste of good scenery to send me through it, since even this AM. I have but the dimmest image of how it really looked. I ought to *write* descriptions of it as I go along, then I should have 'knowledge *about*' it, if not direct sensuous 'acquaintance.' " He referred her to his *Principles of Psychology* (1890) for this distinction. (8:69-71) That same day he wrote Swiss psychologist Théodore Flournoy: "It has made me understand the vastness of my dear native land better than I ever did before." (8:71) He stayed another night, likely indulging in the nearby hot mineral springs vapor caves.

On 15 August he headed east via Leadville. At Divide (9,160 feet) in a "shanty with tarred paper and battened over the boards outside to keep out the rain & wind," he might not have expected the supper to be "spotlessly clean, appetizing and good," but that was what was served. And the view: "the most exquisite pale green and gray tints to where the violet serrations of the mountains frame in the horizon," he wrote Henry. After supper, he rode three miles from the station "in the starlight on top of a 6-horse stage" to Cripple Creek, where on the morning of the 16th he inspected a mine, "climbing down slippery stairs with the water dripping all over you, 400 feet below the surface." (2:373-375) That night he started across the continent, arriving in Boston at 3 PM on 19 August.

Back at Chocorua, 22 August, he wrote Elizabeth Goddard a thank-you: "For me change of scenery and life is a vital necessity without which I go out like a fire that is n't [sic] poked. I regret it, for if there is anything I *aspire* to, it is to be able to work steadily on day after day with no need of change, but my bad nervous temperament keeps me exiled from that Eden." Imagine how even more prodigious his output would have been had he been able to work in this fashion, though we would miss letters like this, which closed, "Colorado has now become a part of my Self." (8:74)

INFINITE GOOD

A FINE TEN DAYS IN KEENE VALLEY

❧

2 -14 (?) September 1895, *Adirondacks*
Gothics, 4,736 *feet*

"The company is first rate, and the walking day after day does one infinite good," William wrote, urging a colleague to come to the Adirondacks. (8:77)

After returning from Colorado on 19 August, James did not linger long at either of his two homes. "I bless you day and night and my gratitude to you for all you have been and are to me, runs over and over," he wrote Alice on eve of his departure. (8:79) Leaving Cambridge at 7:18 A.M. on 30 August 1895, he caught the 8:00 train to Burlington, Vermont. From there he crossed Lake Champlain on the 4:45 ferry to Westport, New York, and from there he traveled by stagecoach to an inn in Elizabethtown. James made a short stay in the Keene Valley, Adirondacks, home of William and Helen Warren, after which the Warrens drove him to the Shanty at Putnam Camp. He arrived at noon on 2 September.

Early the next morning he wrote Alice, "such a heavenly peace & happiness have flooded me since I have been here." (8:81)

Later that day, 3 September, he, Jim Putnam, Dickinson Sergeant Miller, and a fourth headed for the Gothics. From Keene Valley center, the easiest way to reach this "triple-crested mountain, with . . . great slides and bare rock," was via the Johns Brook valley, five miles—and then up 2,360 feet over the 3.71-mile Orebed Brook to the 4,736-foot summit.[1] (The quartet may have gotten a lift at the start of this.) "I strained (not sprained) my *other* ankle in running down the Gothics," he informed Alice on the fifth. A day later, all was healed. (8:81-82, 573)

in this delicious cot among the hills

By 1895 James, had been coming regularly to Keene Valley, one summer after another, for two decades. His first trip, at age thirty-three, was made in 1875. Then he came with three of his former Harvard Medical School friends: the Putnam brothers—James Jackson (neurologist; 1846-1918) and Charles Pickering (physician; 1844-1914)—and Henry Pickering Bowditch (physiologist; 1840-1911). They boarded at Smith Beede's farmhouse at the southeastern end of valley, near the village of St. Huberts. The mountains so captivated them that the next year they bought land from Beede along with his farmhouse and built a Keene Valley eclectic style of small buildings, christened Putnam Camp.[2]

In Keene Valley his relationship with his beloved Alice had bloomed. He had met the former Alice Gibbens in January 1876 in Boston. In late summer 1876 while James stayed at Putnam Camp and Alice lodged at nearby Beede's boardinghouse, he decided that he loved her.[3]

In 1877, they separated for the summer. Alice vacationed in Quebec. James spent six weeks in Keene Valley. He related to her his six-day excursion in "the most perfect weather." This included Indian Pass (2,834 feet)—"the grandest scenery I've seen yet—quite alpine"— and culminated in a crowning climb of Whiteface (4,867 feet)— via trail from Lake Placid under a different sky from last year's—"a perfect vision of beauty"— and a "scramble down through the woods on the other side"—"an arduous six hours tramp" to complete a seven-mile, west-east traverse. They returned by wagon to Beede's. "[L]uxuriating in the benediction of the woods" James was "absolutely renovated and rejuvenated", physically and mentally. (4:584-586)

The next summer was entirely different for William and Alice. On Wednesday morning, 10 July 1878, they were married in the home of her grandmother, Mary Gibbens, at 153 Boylston Street, Boston. That afternoon the newlyweds left for Keene Valley, where the groom had secured the rental of James Putnam's cottage. They traveled there via New York (Windsor Hotel) and Saratoga Springs (Grand Union Hotel) and Lake George (Fort William Henry Hotel) and, as James remembered twenty years later, a rather disappointing sail up the lake.

Their honeymoon lasted ten weeks! Despite much rain, the Jameses took long walks in the woods, though probably not up any mountains, at least no ascents are mentioned in James's correspondence. The letters diminished because his prime pen pal was with him. Upon hearing of his brother's marriage, bachelor Henry in London rejoiced "as if it were my own" and wished he "could pay a visit to your romantic shanty, among those mountains with which you must now be so familiar & which I have never seen."[4] (1:305) On their marriage eve, James had written his brother Bob, "I've no doubt by next September the mountains & my wife will have made me all right again." (5:18) His prophesy was spot on. "We have spent," William described their idyll, "a ballad-like summer in this delicious cot among the hills. We only needed crooks and a flock of sheep." (5:20) There was at least one exalted moment. When Alice returned she was pregnant. She gave birth to Henry James (Harry) on 18 May 1879.

Let's return to James's early September 1895 visit to Putnam Camp, following the Colorado journey. Here he would meet Pauline Goldmark, who would become a significant friend and climbing companion. Goldmark was then a twentiy-one-year-old senior at Bryn Mawr College. Dickinson Sergeant Miller (1868-1963), a friend and a philosophy teacher at Bryn Mawr, introduced James to Goldmark. James wrote Alice: "she climbs cliffs like a monkey in his [Miller's] company."[5] (8:82)

James returned to Cambridge on the night of 15 September 1895.

Several years later, James would write Goldmark: "But you, my dear young friend, are such an up at sunrise, out of door, and mountain-top kind of a girl. (8:517,18 April 1899)

PART TWO

The Green Mountains
of Vermont

※

While traveling to and from the Adirondacks, William James crossed Vermont many times. Yet, the Green Mountains did not call to him the way the Adirondacks and White Mountains did, at least not enough for him to tell us of any climbing experiences.

In 1874 and 1875, James's sister Alice and his aunt Kate (his mother's sister) summered at the Bread Loaf Inn in Ripton, Vermont, in the heart of the northern Green Mountains. James's parents had summered here.[1] In 1874 James spent "only 5 weeks away from home, at a variety of watering places on the coast and for 8 days in the green mountains." (4:503) The "watering places" were Newcastle, New Hampshire, York Harbor, Maine, and the Isles of Shoals, in both Maine and New Hampshire. By the "green mountains," James probably meant those surrounding the Bread Loaf Inn, although he does not verify this. In early July 1875, however, James noted spending four days at the Bread Loaf Inn with Alice and Kate, "very pleasantly," he added. (4:515-517) Again, there is no hint of whether that pleasure included mountain climbing. Yet, knowing of his love of mountains, how could he have resisted?

On 15 July 1874 and 1875 during the Jameses' visits, the innkeeper, Joseph Battell, celebrated his thirty-fifth and thirty-sixth birthdays; he was slightly older than James, at thirty-two and thirty-three. Battell was a native of Middlebury, Vermont, eleven miles west and north of Bread Loaf, a post office created to serve the inn. Battell had studied three years at Middlebury College,1856-1859, although he did not graduate. Instead, for his education and health, he made a two-year walking tour of Europe and Britain, leaving in October 1860 and returning in January 1863.

Battell described this odyssey in his book, *The Yankee Boy from Home* (1864)[2]. In August 1861, he left Geneva with an American couple who had persuaded him to join their tour of Switzerland. First they headed by diligence southeast to Chamonix, stopping at Sallenche (Sallanches). Battell walked the remaining eighteen miles to Chamonix, in constant view of Mont Blanc (15,771 feet). From Chamonix (3,445 feet) he walked across the Glacier of Bossons, ascended Montanvert (6,303 feet), and crossed the Mer de Glace to Jardins. (25-29) (One year earlier, in May 1860, William James had made virtually this same journey with his younger brother Henry.[3] Thus commenced three young men's lives of mountain climbing.)

Moving eastward, Battell and company also ascended Torrenthorn (9,836 feet), at Leuky Bad (Leukerbad), and the popular Rigi (5,906 feet), on the northern shore of Lake Lucerne, where they stayed at the hotel atop and savored the sunset. From a third celebrated viewpoint, La Dôle (5,502 feet), second highest of the Swiss Jura, seven miles north of Nyon, Battell saw Mont Blanc "magnifi-cently" and "the whole lake of Geneva, stretching below, like Lake Champlain, as seen from Bertha Mountain in Vermont."[4] (34)

From Switzerland Battell explored the Pyrenees afoot and alone. "I have been up over seven thousand feet four different times," he claimed when done on 12 September 1861. (44) These heights included Port de Vanasque (7,917 feet), Port de Picard, and Pic des Bergons.

Battell sauntered inn to inn through Scotland, noting hills, heather, sheep, lassies. Each sabbath, he paused for the day and attended church services. At Collander, in the Trossachs ("bristly country"), he learned that the ascent of Ben Ledi (2,873 feet) was six miles. (100) He walked the nine-mile length of Loch Katrine, fourteen miles around Ben More (3,817 feet), and looked across Loch Tay to Ben Lawers (3,984 feet), "a giant mountain, an enormous sheep-pasture." He skirted the foot of Britain's highest, Ben Nevis (4,406 feet), at Fort William.(123) The ascent most etched in his memory: the scene from atop Ben Lomand (3,192 feet). (136)

His Ireland sojourn took him south. He did not traverse England's Lake District of the Cumbrian Mountains, of William Wordsworth fame, as we might expect. (As we shall see, William James will visit the Lake District in 1908.) From Dublin, Battell crossed St. George's Channel to Wales. As seen from Holyhead Mountain, at 700 feet the highest place on the Welsh isle of Anglesey, the Welsh mountains reminded Battell of Vermont's Green Mountains. He climbed Wales's highest mountain, Snowden (3,571 feet).

Finding no forests or mountains abroad that compared with Vermont's, Battell cherished those of his homeland all the more and sounded this prophetic note: "Would that the day might never come when our mountains shall lose their greatness, or America her woods and forests!" (104-105) The year 1870 was the "height of deforestation," in Vermont, observed historian Jan Albers: "about 70 percent of Vermont was cleared and 30 percent was forested."[5] Today those figures are reversed. The fact that nearly three-quarters of Vermont is now green can be attributed in part to Joseph Battell. At the suggestion of his school friend Ezra Brainerd, later president of Middlebury College (1885-1906), Battell went to Ripton, Vermont. What he found there nourished his soul. As a result, in April 1866, he purchased a farmhouse on 300 acres, which he opened as a public house that summer. To this acquisition, he added a stretch of some sixty miles of Green Mountains from Brandon northward to Waterbury . (Was he inspired by the Marquis of Breadalbane whose lands mostly of "mountain and rock"—some of which Battell traversed—encompassed some thirty-six by ninety miles in Scotland?) In 1910, he gave Camels Hump to the people of Vermont. In 1915 he willed 30,000 acres to Middlebury College. This great gift also included the inn, now home to Middlebury College's Bread Loaf School of English and Writers' Conference.[6]

Battell's preservation of the Green Mountains needs to be celebrated perennially. In December 2006 the New England Wilderness Act designated the Joseph Battell Wilderness of 12,300 acres, through which the Long Trail passes for nine miles, from Brandon Gap to the Middlebury Snow Bowl.[7] Battell's vision places him in the pantheon of American conservationists.

Two and a half miles eastward from the Bread Loaf Inn, the Long Trail crosses Route 125 at the Middlebury Gap (2,149 feet). In the late summer of 1922, the poet Robert Frost camped here at Lake Pleiad awaiting his hiking companions.

Like James, Frost was drawn to the mountains of northern New England.[8] He had grown up following his father's and mother's footsteps up and down the hills of San Francisco, where he was born in 1874. (We will find William James walking the same hills in 1898.) After Frost's father's death from tuberculosis in 1885, the family moved to New England.

In September 1897, Frost, then twenty-four, enrolled as a freshman at Harvard. His father had graduated with honors from Harvard in 1872. Inspired by William James, whose *The Will to Believe* had been released in April of 1897, Frost looked forward to studying with the professor. However, when the opportunity arose in his second year, fall 1898, to take William James's course, Frost's hopes were dashed. After returning from California, 22 September, James was fully engaged teaching Philosophy 9 (Metaphysics) for Josiah Royce, who was preparing to give the Gifford Lectures at Aberdeen and Edinburgh, Scotland, in 1899 and 1900. (8:334n2) Professor Hugo Munsterberg taught the psychology part of the year-long General Introduction to Philosophy in which Frost was enrolled; the class used as text James's *Psychology: Briefer Course* (1892). Meanwhile, that fall of 1898, James, too, was to concentrate on his own Gifford Lectures—still over a year away[9]—but made little headway until, he reflected, it was "communicated to me, by divine inspiration, of not doing anything for anybody else . . . on any day until I should have done at least one hour of work *for myself*. If you spend your time preparing to be ready, you *never* will be ready." (8:461)

On 31 March 1899, Frost withdrew from Harvard, not completing the academic year. Family concerns were foremost: he and his wife were expecting a second child in less than a month (Daughter Lesley, who was born 28 April 1899). "My greatest inspiration, when I was a student," Frost would say years later of James, "was a man whose classes I never attended."[10]

Meanwhile, in 1922, Frost's daughter Lesley, then twenty-three, would serve as the catalyst for the Long Trail expedition that found Frost camped in Middlebury Gap. Lesley wanted the Frosts to be the first group to walk the entire Long Trail at one time. The Long Trail was conceived in 1910 to run the entire length of the state of Vermont; in 1922, it reached from the Massachusetts border as far north as Smuggler's Notch in Johnson. Frost and Lesley were joined by Frost's son Carol, twenty; youngest daughter, Marjorie, seventeen; her high school friend, Lillian LaBatt, sixteen, and Edward Ames Richards, a June Amherst College graduate, whose poetry Frost had encouraged. The party of six started on Tuesday, 15 August 1922, from the Frost home, Stone Cottage, in South Shaftsbury, Vermont, each packing "two blankets, a heavy sweater, and a poncho." No tents, no sleeping bags. Frost, himself, at forty-eight, wore a new pair of custom-made alpine shoes, which proved to be his nemesis. Yet, happily botanizing, he followed the others.

From Stone Cottage they walked due east, crossing over Bald Mountain (2,857 feet), 3.5 miles, then descended the east side, on an "indistinct and poorly blazed trail" to Hell Hollow for the night. The next day—their first on the Long Trail which originated 17.5 miles south at the Massachusetts line—they hiked 7.2 miles to top of Glastenbury (3,748 feet) and moved on to the vicinity of Grout Pond. Their third-day camp was near the top of Stratton (3,936 feet). On the fourth day, 18 August, as they reached the Manchester-Londonderry Road (Routes 30 & 11), inclement weather threatened. They took the road three miles east, arriving in a thunderstorm at the Russell Inn in Peru. This was somewhat familiar country to Frost for he and professor Charles Lowell Young of Wellesley College had hiked it in summer 1918. Here the party stayed two nights, giving Frost's feet a needed rest from his uncomfortable footwear. At this point, Frost announced his adjournment, promising to rejoin the others at Middlebury Gap, after he had replaced boots with sneakers. Having had his fill of the Long Trail, Richards exited with Frost.

Refreshed (two nights in a Rutland hotel) and sneakered, Frost arrived in Middlebury by train and walked and hitched to Lake Pleid on Wednesday 23 August, passing the Bread Loaf School of English where he had made his first appearance the previous summer. Gladdened by the company of the youngsters, Frost hiked the Long Trail north 17.3 miles to Lincoln Gap, passing over the Battell (3,482 feet) and Bread Loaf (3,835 feet) mountains. At Lincoln Gap, Frost, his knee aching and still not able to keep pace, decided to leave the younger set once again. He walked the roads 4.7 miles east to Warren and then forty-four miles north through Waterbury and Stowe to Morrisville; he continued eight miles east to Wolcott from which he entrained to Littleton, New Hampshire, to meet his wife, on Monday 4 September. The Frosts continued on to Franconia for the remainder of summer at a "hay feverless altitude."

The others succeeded in traversing the rest of the trail, 71.1 miles, over its highest peaks—Abraham (4,006 feet), Camels Hump (4,083 feet), Mansfield (4,393 feet), finishing in Johnson on 2 September. They figured they had walked "between 220 and 225 miles" in seventeen days (not counting their rest day in Peru), averaging 13.2 miles a day. They endured one day of rain, a thunderstorm. No insects bothered them. They existed on "bread, butter, eggs, shredded wheat, raisins, crackers, rice and sugar . . . cookies and candy" bought at market.[11] They claimed they were the first group to walk the length of the Long Trail in one continuum.

Frost himself had walked two sections of the Long Trail: the first, of 36.9 miles, and the second of 18.1 miles, for a total of fifty-five miles. After the hike, Carol and Lillian became engaged; they married in the fall of 1923. Frost's wedding present to them was his South Shaftsbury farm. Eight years later, in 1930, the Long Trail reached its northern destination, the Canadian border; its length now, according to the 2011 *Long Trail Guide*, is 272.7 miles.

Frost is an icon of this place. Consider: his long association with the Bread Loaf School of English and the Bread Loaf Writers' Conference; his 1924 Middlebury College honorary degree, and his 1939 purchase of the Homer Noble Farm in Ripton, which became his summer home until his death in 1963, and is now a National Historic Landmark.[12] There is also Frost Mountain (2,513 feet), between Middlebury and the Long Trail—so designated by the Vermont state legislature in 1955, in celebration of the man they proclaimed their poet laureate in 1961.

These Alps are absolutely

MEDICINAL

🙢🙠

Switzerland: 1880, 1892-1893

1880

As we have seen, William James began his mountain climbing with brother Henry in Switzerland in 1860.

In the "wunderschoner thaufrischer morgen"—very beautiful, dew-fresh morning—of 29 July 1880, William James, now thirty-eight, departed Interlaken, Switzerland. There he had prepared himself with short climbs before traveling seven miles west (he didn't say how) to Beatenberg (3,773 feet), where he savored the spectacular views of Lake Thun for three days. (5:130) From nearby Interlaken he traveled southeast by "post wagen," for three and a half hours to Grindelwald (3,394 feet), in the heart of the Bernese Oberland, where in July 1872 brother Henry had climbed the Faulhorn (8,796 feet)[1].

From Grindelwald at 1:00 in the afternoon, William James walked with a porter carrying his newly acquired canvas valise over the Grosse Scheideck (or Scheidegg; 6,434 feet) and down three miles to a small chalet for the night.[2] There from in his "little wooden bedroom" he wrote Alice: "I really love this Switzerland more and more every moment and last night had emotions about it which I have n't [sic] had for years." While writing, he observed "an avalanche thunders on the Wetterhorn [12.142 feet] opposite whose silver grey sides & Ice covered top we have been skirting all the afternoon." The next morning at six he: "trudged mainly down hill through lovely scenery to a place called Imhof (near Meyringen [Meiringen, 1,969 feet])". Here he noted enjoying a "good long nap." Then at mid-afternoon he walked south, rain halting him for an hour—"up hill all the way"—to Guttannen. (5:127-129)

The next day, 31 July, James continued walking and riding south to Handeck (Handegg) for an "enormous" breakfast, which he did not describe. Then onto Grimsel Hospice for lunch and rest, "the high and distant prospect was destroyed by low hanging clouds." James continued his journey "enveloped in cold cloud up to the summit of the desolate pass" (7,103 feet). From there he had a "stupendous steep down view of Rhone Glacier & valley, Furca pass" (7,976 feet). Down he "ran to the single house which forms the settlement," from which he wrote to reassure Alice of his condition. "Don't be afraid of my over doing things. I know from my Adirondack experience that this sort of thing with resting intervals does me the greatest good." (5:128-129)

On 1 August James walked over the Furka Pass, before boarding a stage east to Andermatt (4,713 feet) for the night.

"I am getting along splendidly," he exuded to Henry in a short letter of 2 August—"a most unforgettable day in the Banquette through the Vorder Rhein Thal" to Reichenau for night. At Reichenau the two branches of the Rhine merge; the Vorderrhein from west and the Hinterrhein from south become Alpenrhein, which flows north to Lake Constance. The next morning the stage brought James south to Thusis from which he walked to Splügen for the night. (1:324) He left on foot at six on the cold morning of 4 August, surmounting the Splügen Pass (6,933 feet). The "keenness" of the north wind "perfectly intoxicated" him. Snow on both sides of pass "slightly powdered" him. The "blue sky broke ahead" and James proceeded "in a flood of sunlight down the tremendous terraces of the almost vertical road" until the stage met him. By two o'clock he was in "paradise"—Bellagio, Lake Como, Italy.

The Splügen appears to be James's last ascent during this trip, or at least that he mentions in his correspondence of the period. James kept on the move, however: Milan by train to Lake Maggiore, and a five-hour diligence ride in the rain to Domodossola for night. Saturday 7 August held "prospects of fine day for walk," though "coming down to low air makes me feel less rejuvenated physically than I had supposed." Unable to resist the pull of Zermatt, James journeyed from Visp on horseback for four hours and by wagon for three. His eyes, he wrote to Alice from Zermatt, kept him "from settling in a quiet way in one place." In this 8 August letter, he said, "I think I've got the effect of the Alps as much as will do me good and I'd better stop the walking, or I'll lose the benefit." (5:133) He turned homeward though Geneva, Chambéry, Paris, London.

1892

On 25 May 1892 William James left the United States to spend his Harvard sabbatical abroad with his wife and children. James passed the summer of 1892 in Switzerland, going hither and yon to find schooling for sons, Harry and Billy. Despite these challenges, James still managed to tramp about the mountains. In August, he made a ten-day (eight-day, he told another) trip alone to the Engadine—the valley of the Inn in eastern Switzerland—about which he gave no detail. (7:308, 310) After this he traveled to Chamonix, France, at the base of Mont Blanc, where on 17 August he ascended Brévent (8,285 feet), "steep & steady, but with a view which paid for all," he wrote Alice. "These Alps are absolutely medicinal, and I can well understand the passion growing for higher, higher, if the strength w[oul]d only grow in proportion." (7:314)

Greatly refreshed James enthused: Switzerland is "an unmitigated blessing, from the mountains down to the bread and butter and the beds." (7:297) "It meets all the major needs of body and soul as no other country does, in summer time," he wrote a Swiss friend. (7:322) With summer drawing to a close, the Jameses departed for Italy, to winter in Florence, from which there were no reports of mountain climbing.

1893

Come spring, in mid-April 1893, James left Florence for Switzerland. Alice joined him in Lucerne where they settled in nearby Meggen until late May. On Sunday 21 May—the day after brother Henry departed, following a three-week visit—William ascended the Righi (or Rigi, 5,906 feet), spending the night atop. *Baedeker's* called it: "the most famous mountain viewpoint in Switzerland." At four o'clock the next morning the trumpet awoke him only to "gaze upon a dense cloud fog which lasted till nine." With the "view half cleared," he "had a perfectly delicious walk of two hours along the ridge of the mountain to Righi-Scheidegg [5,463 feet], no human being any where in sight, and the soft strong air blowing in my face and keeping things cool, and hence down hill two hours more to Gersau and home by boat." (2:267-268) All this he wrote Henry on 24 May. Henry had himself climbed there twenty-four years earlier.[3]

James arrived in Vers-chez-les-Blanc above Lausanne on 24 July, his main residence until 18 August. During this time James took his two oldest sons on an eight-day walking tour (3-11 August), which included ascents of Gornergrat (10,270 feet) and Riffelberg (8,472 feet) from Zermatt on 7 August, "a glorious 10 hours," five of which were walking "with no great exertion" in "the very perfection of weather and sublimity." On 10 August from Hotel Jungfrau, they rose to the 9,636-foot top of Eggishorn before returning to their hotel for a 9:30 breakfast. Then they walked over Riederalp (6,398 feet) and Belalp (6,824 feet) on their way down to Brig (2,244 feet) before arriving back where they started. (7:450, 2:274)

"Had I the power, I should never want to go out of Switzerland for my summers," he wrote Henry on 28 July. (2:272)

William James and John Muir had come close to crossing paths in summer 1893. On 10 June Muir toured Cambridge, partly with Josiah Royce, James's Harvard colleague and neighbor. On 7 August Muir was in London, while James was on heights just mentioned. On 14 August Muir spent the night at the Hotel Gibbon in Lausanne, before moving to Zermatt the next day and the Gornergrat the next, where James had been nine days earlier.[4]

On 18 August James departed Switzerland "with a tragic sort of regret that I say good bye to this place . . . on the whole the most faultless country that I know, and the most beauteous, for some thing tells me rather solemnly that I shall most likely never return again." (7:457) He arrived in Cambridge on 5 September.

The White Mountains
of New Hampshire
and the Adirondacks

꙾

1896–1897

In early August 1896, William and Alice James traveled by coach and team from the Intervale train station in North Conway, New Hampshire, to Stonehurst, the English-style summer home of Daniel and Helen Bigelow Merriman.

Helen Merriman's father, Erastus Brigham Bigelow, a Boston carpet magnate, had commissioned the Boston architecture firm of Snell and Gregson to design and construct Stonehurst in 1871 and 1872. Destroyed by fire in 1875, the Victorian home was rebuilt and reoccupied in September 1877. Two years later Bigelow died at age sixty-five, leaving Stonehurst to his only child, Helen. During much of 1895, the year prior to the Jameses' visit, she had orchestrated the refurbishment and enlargement of the main building.[1] Today Stonehurst is advertised as "The Premiere White Mountain Boutique Hotel."

Helen had married Daniel Merriman twenty-two years earlier, on 1 September 1874, four years before Alice and William James had wed. The Merrimans had no children. At the time of the Jameses' visit, Daniel, fifty-eight, was pastor of the Central Congregational Church in Worcester, Massachusetts, a position he had held since 1878. Helen, fifty-two, had studied art with William Morris Hunt in his Boston studio. There she met Sarah Wyman Whitman and the two became close friends. Helen recommended that Whitman make the stained-glass windows for her husband's church. Helen and Daniel helped to found the Worcester Museum of Art, which was incorporated in February 1896 and opened in 1898. Both were original trustees. At the wishes of its benefactor, Stephen Salisbury III, Daniel became the Museum's first president, serving until his death in 1912. Helen continued on the board until 1923. Her portrait by Cecilia Beaux hangs in the Museum.[2]

The Jameses appreciated the generous views that Stonehurst offers: it looks west towards Mount Washington, New England's highest ground, and east into a second-growth forest of hemlock, white pine, beech, red oak, red maple, and red spruce, which rises steeply to the summit of Bartlett Mountain (2,661 feet) on the western shoulder of Kearsarge North (3,268 feet). In 1914 Helen gave some of her land to the state of New Hampshire for the Merriman State Forest.[3]

During the Jameses' stay with the Merrimans, even a New England heat wave—Boston reported a hundred degrees—did not deter William from making two ascents.

The first was not described. The second was from the top of Washington (6,288 feet) "over the backs," of the Northern Presidential Range, he wrote brother Henry, (2:406-407). How he reached the summit is not disclosed. Perhaps the Merrimans drove him, at least as far as Glen House, 16.5 miles north of their home, where he may have hired a taxi for the eight-mile-road trip to the summit.

The Presidentials that William traversed were all above treeline: Clay (5,533 feet; Henry Clay was never a US president), Jefferson (5,716 feet), and Adams (5,799 feet). This traverse, of about six miles total, plus side trails to the summits, requires three-and-a-half hours, according to the *White Mountain Guide.* The first edition of this indispensable vade mecum, appearing in 1907, was not available to James. His lunch on Mount Adams upset his system. One wonders what he ate. He "had a bad three hours getting down through the woods in state of active nausea & diarrhea." It is likely that his descent followed the Great Gulf Wilderness on the Madison Gulf Trail: it would have taken five miles to reach the road and then another two miles to reach the Glen House. The vertical relief between Adams and Glen House is 4,236 feet, and includes a headwall.

"But it was a good day all the same," William concluded to Henry. This is the only commentary I found, alas. In such condition William's survival is a blessing, let alone his waxing lyric about plants and vistas.

The haze only made the landscape more poetic,
complex and mysterious

In August 1897, returning from a Down East visit with the
Dorrs at Bar Harbor on Mount Desert, James stopped at
Stonehurst. There he met French psychologist Charles-
Robert Richet, with whom he had corresponded for over a
decade, and Swiss-born psychiatrist Adolf Meyer of Clark
University. On Sunday morning 15 August, the Merriman's
son Roger, who had completed his BA at Harvard the previous year and his MA that year, rowed James and Meyer
across the Saco River.[4] From there they "walked to the
Humphreys ledge place [1,510 feet] going over it from the
opening at this end and coming out where we went the
other day. It had much less glamour than it had then, and
we need not think of it more," James wrote, sharing his
disappointment with his wife. (8:293)

The next day's journey was much to his liking. James
and Richet mounted Washington's west side by the cog
railway and then "had a perfectly magnificent descent" by
the bridle path. They went on foot, not on horseback, following the Crawford Path, down 8.2 miles to the north
end of Crawford Notch. "The haze only made the landscape more poetic, complex and mysterious," James wrote
the Merrimans the next day from Chocorua, seventeen
miles southwest from Intervale. "Richet seemed greatly
impressed by the whole affair." And James, who believed
that "the only way to know a man well is to have a whole
day with him in the open air," found Richet "a most lovable
fellow." (8:294, 601) The Merrimans were the "right sort"
of friends, James wrote Alice, especially spiritually. (8:307)

Two and a half years later, from 21 January to 2 April

1900, Alice and William "wintered" at Richet's lovely château at Carquéranne, in Costebelle, France, close to the Mediterranean coast. They made excursions to nearby Hyères and farther west, to Toulon. Here their spirits rose and William's health improved.[5]

I am thankful that I have 'arrived'

Meanwhile, in late August 1897, once reunited with family at Chocorua, William James was ready to lead them upward. Normal time for James to gain the top of Mt. Chocorua (3,500 feet) was three hours. With his four children and their tutor, as was the case this sweet Sunday, 29 August 1897, it took an hour more. "It was 6-year old Tweedy's first climb," he wrote Henry in England. At the summit they all entertained themselves for three hours. William dozed and savored Sarah Orne Jewett's *The Country of the Pointed Firs* (November 1896). They came down the mountain in two and a half hours, Tweedy leading the way. Immediately William wrote Jewett of his "uncontrollable expression of pleasure" with her book. The next day he recommended the novel to Henry "to recall the very taste & fragrance of your native seaside air."[6] (8:296, 3:17)

Alice's absence from the family's alpine excursion prompts my curiosity about her. Did she not want to go? Actually, as Susan Gunter points out in *Alice in Jamesland* (102), Alice "longed to climb Mt. Chocorua, but she feared that her slow pace would hold the others back." True, too, while they were off tramping, Alice relished the solitude and silence. "Alice did work hard," Gunter concludes, "but she enjoyed life in Chocorua."

Finally, on Monday 6 September 1897, Alice made her first ascent. Leaving their home at 9 A.M. she and son Billy, now a teenager taller than his father, toiled upward "to the house (under the peak) at 3 having had many resting times on the way." Then onto the 3,500-foot summit. They had gained 2,920 feet in elevation in five-miles along dirt roads and the Hammond and Liberty trails. (Compare with Monadnock's Half Way House and White Arrow trails which rise 1,656 feet in 2.2 miles.) Her reward was "a wonderful sunset with driving clouds and all the glory of the earth beneath and above us." Too windy to linger they came down and back to the house by moonlight. If necessary they could havespent the night at the Peak House, a three-story hotel erected in 1891 by David Knowles et al a half mile below the summit; there he and his wife looked after as many as twenty-five guests at one time, serving supper and breakfast.

Two days later Alice wrote "Darling William" of her venture. She regretted "somewhat mournfully" all the times when "I might have gone up, but I am thankful that I have 'arrived' even thus late. Some time I want to go with you."[7]

And he with she. The summer before, in mid-July 1896, James, lecturing in Buffalo, had written Alice, "We ought both to get away into the mountains somewhere by ourselves. I wish we *could* go to Keene Valley!" (8:167) Before going on to Chicago, he had a sylvan interlude at the Adirondack Lodge, which did him "immense physical good." (8:189) On 2 September he wrote Alice, "I fully appreciate your inward need of repose." (8:195) And from Keene Valley he mentioned to her "a deeply good-giving long day [16 September] in the woods & on top of Haystack [4,960 feet]." (8:202, 204)

Keene Valley is good for brief and intense periods of climbing.

No sooner was James down from Chocorua's heights than he left Alice on 31 August for Cambridge. From there he departed on 2 September 1897 by train for Burlington, Vermont, where he ferried across Lake Champlain to Westport, New York. He reached his destination, Putnam's Camp, Keene Valley, on Thursday the third. Then followed "a sweet harmonious day at the ponds"—Round, Twin, Bullet—with British statesman James Bryce and his wife, Marion. James Bryce "has penetrated into every corner of the world" William marveled in his letter to Alice, "and remembers the name of every place, and every human being he ever spoke to, in his travels. He is also a botanist and discerns plants at every step. An extraordinary blithe and wholesome being!" (8:298)

On 5 September, an ideal day, William, James Bryce, Felix Adler (whose wife was Helen Goldmark), and James and Charles Putnam switchbacked up the Giant (4,627 feet). "Adler & Bryce kept up conversation, hammer & tongs uninterrupted by the steepest gradients. B. is inimitable—a walking mine of information and good spirits." (8:299) They most likely followed the Roaring Brook trail which left from their doorway and rose 3,375 feet in three and a half miles.

On Tuesday, 7 September, William rose early to see the Bryces off.

———

Twenty-seven years earlier Bryce, then thirty-two, had made the first of his many trips to America. On the dark, rainy night of 3 September 1870, Bryce traveled by buggy southward over a rough mountain road from Gorham, New Hampshire, for seven-and-a-half miles to Glen House in the White Mountains. The young Bryce was of medium stature with reddish beard and reddish brown hair. When he returned to England that November he would be the Regius professor of law at Oxford. Eager to meet Americans and know their culture, laws, politics, arts—everything—Bryce noted the noble visage of one passenger in his late sixties, traveling with his son, who had turned twenty-six that July. He met the Emersons, Waldo and Edward, after arriving at Glen House at 9:00 P.M.[8]

The next day Bryce and Edward strolled "up the Glen and over into Glen Ellis" to find encamped there artist William James Stillman, who was also staying at Glen House. In August 1858 at Follansbee Pond in the Adirondacks Stillman had painted a party of philosophers, Emerson included. The trio had "a delicious bath" in a pool below Glen Ellis Falls before returning to the Glen House, three miles north.[9]

The next morning, 5 September, at eight o'clock, Bryce and Edward began walking up Mount Washington. After four miles, "the wind rises to a tempest," Bryce noted in his journal, and rain makes "things grow generally miserable and hopeless." Here the two separated, Edward joining his father in a stagecoach, while Bryce gained the top "drenched." Drying by the Summit House stove, drinking whiskey to stave off cold and fatigue, they waited an hour for dinner at 1:30. Nourished, they descended the west side, shivering in fog and wind on the open-air cog railway. From the base station they rode by carriage some ten or eleven miles, reaching Crawford House at five o'clock for the night.[10]

The next morning, the 6th, they parted company. The Emersons traveled via stage to Whitefield, then by rail to Plymouth for the night, continuing on by train to Boston and home.

Bryce journeyed to Profile House in Franconia Notch from which he climbed Mount Lafayette (5,260 feet), starting rather late in the afternoon and returning, the last part by moonlight.[11]

———

Meanwhile, back at Putnam Camp, on 8 September 1897, after the Bryces departed, James visited with the Longfellows, Alice and Edith (now Mrs. Richard H. Dana). That warm night "the mystic moonlight flooded the mountains and the valley. This september [sic] moon in this place is surely one of the beauties of the world," James wrote his wife, recalling their 1877 courtship summer when she was in Canada and he, in this "wondrous place." (8:300)

The 10th or 11th—it's unclear from his letters—James spent alone on Noonmark. After a two-mile, 2,000-foot climb from the Ausable Golf Club (which is across Highway 73 from Putnam Camp) via Stimson Trail, William rested atop the 3,556-foot mountain. Happily, under clear skies he read one hundred pages of an unnamed book and communed with nature. "I can hardly live away from your sweetness," he wrote Alice. "I wish you could come here for one more day, and we go up noonmark [sic] together, which is much less work than Chocorua." (8:301-303) Had he heard of her ascent of their mountain? Yet, an irony of their separations was that it brought them both peace. (8:305)

"The society here is absolutely sedative," he wrote Alice. "[O]ne settles down into it as into a family." Adapting somewhat to the situation he felt kept him "more flexible and young." "[T]his complete simplification and detachment from every suggestion of responsibility, is what will help me most towards next winter's work." (8:302)

James spent the 16th with Pauline Goldmark and company on Hopkins, three trail miles north of the Giant. Hopkins, at 3,183 feet, is slightly taller than Monadnock and shorter than Chocorua. There are two trails from Keene Valley Highway 73. Since one is rarely used according to the ADK guide, we can see them on the Mossy Brook Trail for three miles and a 2,120-foot elevation gain. "A beautiful dreamy day," he wrote Alice. "Miss G.[oldmark] is at her best in the woods, where she is a perfect deer." (8:306)

That concluded his Keene Valley season for the year. For Alice, he summed up his time there: "Keene Valley is good for brief and intense periods of climbing." (8:602).

"All this society does me no good," William wrote. Yet he had made commitments to Ida and Henry Lee Higginson, with whom he spent three nights, at their Lake Champlain estate, Rock Harbor, in Westport, New York, before driving to Thomas Davidson's in Hurricane. By September's end he had made his way back home to Cambridge.

The *biggest* TRAMP I EVER TOOK!

※

Adirondacks 1898

"I have been in the open air and effulgent light all day"

William James wrote these words to Alice the night of 23 June 1898, having sailed up Lakes George and Champlain. He had set sail at 8:30 A.M. from the village of Caldwell at the south end of Lake George, recalling their 1878 honeymoon at the nearby Fort William Henry Hotel (1855). Ten hours later he disembarked at the Hotel Champlain (now part of Clinton Community College), Bluff Point, south of Plattsburgh, New York. His accommodations and their setting impressed him. "The grounds are laid out by some first class landscape gardener, and present a perfectly beautiful set of effects. I haven't seen anything like it in America." (8:378) Shortly after it opened in June 1890, Hotel Champlain appeared on the cover of *Harper's Weekly* of 16 August 1890.

The hotel's architect was Charles Harney of New York and the "first class landscape gardener" was Charles Miller, superintendent of grounds for Philadelphia's Fairmount Park.

The next day James lingered to further absorb "the beauties of this place." Over four hundred acres beckoned him. They included, "landscaped parks, formal walkways and paths, carriage drives, wooded lawns, bridle paths, wooded tracts, and lakeshore . . . known as the 'Beach of Singing Sands,' " according to professor Bryant F. Tolles Jr.[1]

Leaving mid-afternoon, James made a "loitering journey through a very desolate country," traveling west by train and stage coach to the Grand View Hotel, Lake Placid. Again he wrote Alice. "The scenery looks beautiful this morning,—a strong S.W wind ruffling all things, a sky of melting blue and white, and lake and mountain outlines and all things fitted to rebaptize one into purity and health." (8:379)

On 25 July, Henry Van Hoevenberg once again welcomed William at the Adirondack Lodge. This time, at least at the beginning, leisure prevailed. James was "perfectly happy to let the days slide by one by one." He walked an hour to the Ausable River and an hour back with "little Mr. Van, with his leather clothes, his high heeled boots, his knife, his hatchet and his pistol at his belt, just like a person in a story-book." William was the only guest in this "absolute *sanctuary*; never was such a feeling of peace and security known." (8:382-383)

The end of June his sedentary spell was broken. James ascended "Macintire Mountain"—"3 hours up, two down, with a stiff wind on top from the SE." This is Algonquin

(5,114 feet), the highest peak of the MacIntyre Range, as it is now known, 4.3 miles from the lodge. The next day, 1 July, he rested: "Somewhat stiff from yesterday's climb." Then late in the afternoon, James climbed Mount Jo (2,876 feet). After supper he watched from the lodge's tower the "beautiful solemn scene, with its cool breath, the sky almost cloudless, and the moon hanging above Marcy," he wrote Alice. (8:387)

On 5 July, he walked from Heart Lake through Avalanche Pass to Lake Colden and back, "twice 7 miles or more," having "rarely seen the forest more beautiful or enjoyed it more." (8:389) The Adirondack Mountain Club Guide says the distance one-way is 6.1 miles.

The biggest *tramp* I ever took!

After a rest day, James was ready for Mount Marcy. With "a first-rate guide to carry the baggage," James had only to heft his eighteen-pound pack. (8:615) They departed the lodge at 7:00 in the morning and reached the top at noon. At four that afternoon they descended the southeast side to Panther Gorge Camp, "an hour's walk," to join Pauline and Charles Goldmark and four associates. James described the night as "one of the most memorable of all my memorable experiences." He was "not aware of sleeping at all," while the others "slept without moving an eyelash" by their huge fire. The sky clear, the wind still, the moon appeared before midnight. James entered into "a state of spiritual alertness of the most vital description." Calling this "Walpurgis nacht," James recalled the celebration involving witches congregating on the eve of 1 May, the saint's day of the German abbess Walpurgis. To James it "seemed as if the gods of all the nature-mythologies were holding an indescribable meeting in my breast with the moral gods of the inner life." In a letter to Alice, he concluded, "[i]t was one of the happiest lonesome nights of my existence." However he did not elaborate concerning its significance.

At six the next morning, 8 July, the sleepless James departed for Marcy and was the first to reach the top, the others following in half an hour. Then came "10½ hours of the solidest walking I ever made," James reflected in a letter to Alice the next morning. Down Marcy, up and down Bason Mountain, "away down and up the Gothics, not counting a third down and up over an intermediate spur." Arriving at Putnam Camp in Saint Huberts at 8:00 that evening, James was "more fatigued than I have been after a walk." He slept soundly and well in his old room. (8:390-391, 393-394)

"You always use yourself up in the Adirondacks," Alice responded to her husband's *biggest* tramp." (8:395)

Next James moved to the Willey House (Mountain House) on East Hill, at the edge of the beautiful Keene Valley on the north. His purpose was to see friends at the Glenmore School of the Culture Sciences, just up the road from the Mountain House, at the base of Hurricane Mountain. Among them was Glenmore's founder, the Scottish-American, bachelor-scholar Thomas Davidson, "a great big dynamo who emits sparks, makes things red hot, magnetizes wires," as James described him to Alice, James appreciated Davidson's lecture on Manichean philosophy. [2] (8:392)

James had visited the area the prior September. He had stayed at Willey House, seen Davidson, whose "dining room-kitchen-store house-laundry building was burnt" and "still glowing," following the devastating house fire. On this same visit James had purchased acreage known as the "Moore Land" nearby. (8:300, 302, 304)

On 10 July 1898, James strolled about his recently-acquired land with Dickinson Sergeant Miller, who was also staying at the Willey House, and whose enthusiasm for the territory exceeded James's. Waking at 3 A.M. on 16 July, James decided to see some of his land at sunrise. So he climbed the nearby Little Crow Mountain (not quite a mile from the road) to its 2,459-foot summit, where he spent "a most enjoyable 4 hours." He bought an additional seven acres for $600. (8:392, 396, 616)

Arriving back to Cambridge on 21 July, James had only a week at home before leaving for California. "The foliage is certainly more perfect and heavy this summer than I have ever seen it," he noted to his son Henry James III. "Each individual elm-leaf is dark and glossy and clean like an orange leaf." (8:399)

MY COMPLETEST UNION

WITH MY NATIVE LAND

⁂

The Sierra Nevada of California, 1898

"That summer, when we walked over the 'range' together and I went to California to 'talk to teachers,' marked my completest union with my native land," William James wrote in a 22 October 1908 letter to Pauline Goldmark. (12:110) He was recalling his first experience of the Sierra Nevada range a decade earlier.

In mid-summer 1898, James traveled west by train through Canada.[1] After a "most delicious night of slumber," at the Windsor Hotel in Montreal, James climbed Mount Royal (763 feet) on 29 July, his umbrella shielding him from 86-degree sun. "I lay most comfortably under a big maple in the tangled wilderness of the summit, and let the warm SW. wind flow over me, and was visited by most sweet expositions of sleep." (8:402)

He next stretched his legs in the Canadian Rockies. Yet during his walks from the Banff Springs Hotel (1888) at 5,680 feet "up a near hill with a bridle path" at night and again in the early morning, he felt uncomfortable with the "wild & barren, but in many ways awfully beautiful scene." "[The] whole thing is so inhuman and hostile to life," he wrote Alice. (8:403)

Here James encountered the sublime. James's words about Banff echo those of Thoreau about Katahdin (5,267 feet), Maine's highest ground, collected posthumously in his book, *The Maine Woods* (1864). For on 7-8 September 1846, Thoreau came face to face with "Vast, Titanic, inhuman Nature." Thoreau wrote: "Nature was here something savage and awful, though beautiful. . . . There was there felt the presence of a force not bound to be kind to man." (64, 70)[2]

James's journey from Banff to Seattle was "a stupendous affair—perfectly tremendous scenery almost all the time, and a good deal of variety in it too." (8:404) However, forest fires filled the air with heat and smoke; this was likely the reason he did not mention Mount Rainier (14,410 feet). James spent 12 hours in Seattle (5:30 P.M. to 5:00 A.M.), 5-6 August. But he does not mention any of its seven hills, not even the highest, Queen Anne, at 456 feet.[3] He wrote Alice that "poor Seattle, with a couple of streets of fine business blocks, is surrounded by rawness unspeakable." (8:405) This was changing, however, at the very moment of his witness. As he rested at the Rainier Hotel, the Klondike gold rush was in full swing.

James traveled down the Pacific Coast through Oregon into California, where "Mount Shasta [14,162 feet] was hardly visible for the smoke, till we got round to this southern side of it, which proved to be the seat of fire and the smoke's source." (8:407)

San Francisco Hills

James arrived in San Francisco at 8:30 on Wednesday morning, 10 August. He stayed at the Occidental Hotel at the corner of Montgomery and Bush streets— where his younger brother, Garth Wilkinson James (Wilky), had stayed with Emerson in April and May 1871. The hotel's architecture failed: "Hideous vast stuccoed thing, with long undulating balustrades and wells and lace curtains," William wrote Henry. But he noted: "The fare is very good." (3:39)

That first evening he walked, with some cable car assistance "in the glorious sunset and twilight to the highest hill tops of the city." He might have circled clockwise, reaching Nob Hill (376 feet) in six blocks; then Russian Hill (294 feet); Telegraph Hill (284 feet), north and east; and then down Montgomery Street three-quarters of a mile back to his hotel. Farther afield were Mount Davidson (938 feet), five miles from his hotel, and the Twin Peaks (900+ feet), a mile farther north. Likely his stroll did not encompass these heights for their distance was prohibitive in the alotted time between dinner and 8:15 P.M., when he would return to his lodging. His urban hill-walking, vigorously steep, ups and downs, provided aerobic exercise as well as spectacular views of bay and ocean in three directions and of the San Bruno Mountains (1,314 feet) on the southern edge.[4] (8:406, 409)

Alice knew whereof her husband sauntered. In 1855-1857, she had lived in California with her parents, on a ranch in the northern Santa Clara Valley, near Mountain

View, which lies between Palo Alto, at the southern end of San Francisco Bay, and San Jose. Today the area is known as Silicon Valley. The Santa Cruz Mountains, reaching 3,806 feet, stood between them and the Pacific.

During one magical day in 1856, then seven-year-old Alice walked on Telegraph Hill with California's leading botanist, Albert Kellogg. Both were New England transplants. He had arrived in Sacramento the year of her birth, 1849, with a MD degree from Transylvania University in Kentucky, and with a passion for plants and their medicinal remedies. The forty-three-year-old bachelor enjoyed showing Alice the flora of San Francisco. Three years earlier, on 4 April 1853, he and six others had founded the California Academy of Natural Sciences. In the Academy's *Proceedings* of 7 May 1855 he and Hans Hermann Behr described the giant sequoias of the Sierra Nevada.[5]

―――

Meanwhile, during James's 1898 California sojourn, on Friday 12 August 1898, James, accompanied by the young philosopher Charles Montague Bakewell, journeyed east by train from San Francisco to Raymond for the night. The next day James was awestruck by the "novel and picturesque" scenery, especially "the noblest timber I ever saw," in "every foot" of their forty-four-mile-stage-ride to Wawona at 4,012 feet on the South Fork of Merced River. "The hotel [1879] here is clean & sweet & tasteful, and I have had a splendid bath, & good dinner," he wrote Alice. (8:409-410) Albert Henry Washburn was in charge of the hotel.[6]

On 14 August, from the Wawona Hotel James and Bakewell sauntered eight miles to the Mariposa Sequoias (6,810 feet), gaining 2,790 feet in elevation, and another three miles among these "beauties. . . of magnificent strength and symmetry." The hotel stage brought them back at six o'clock.

———

Earlier Wawona had been known as Clark's Station, for the guardian of the big trees, Galen Clark. On 10-12 May 1871, Clark had escorted Emerson and Muir to Mariposa on horseback. Muir taught Emerson to identify western trees. The "noblest," sugar pine (*Pinus lambertiana*), offered "the best of sweets—better than maple sugar," Muir believed. Growing with the "priests of pines" are other "giants"—the yellow pines (*Pinus ponderosa*) and silver firs (*Abies concolor*), Muir wrote later in *The Mountains of California*. Emerson left Mariposa at 3 P.M. on Friday 12 May, reaching Clark's Station in an hour, from which at five o'clock, he departed by stage en route to San Francisco. Muir slept that night with the sequoias.[7]

———

"Another of the good out-of-door days of my life," exclaimed James on 15 August 1898 at Wawona. He and Bakewell walked, "with books in our pockets and lunch in our hands, to a certain waterfall or series of waterfalls 4 miles long, beginning a couple of miles from the house." Chilnualna Falls severely reduced due to draught disappointed James. Yet the eponymous creek quenched their thirst, "and the day was noble." They "climbed some 4 miles up the mountain side, lying down and reading at several places . . ." It appears that they followed the creek northeast towards the Chilnualna Lakes, attaining an estimated 8,000 feet. The mountain—its flora, immense pines, rocks, air "sizzling hot" with the "aromatic scent of the hamamelis [genus for witch-hazel] bear-clover carpet"—was all new to him.[8] (8:411)

Traveling over the South Fork Road from Wawona (opened 22 July 1875), James and Bakewell arrived at the Sentinel Hotel in Yosemite Valley at noon on 16 August.[9]

———

Twenty-seven years earlier, in May 1871, Emerson and entourage (including Wilky James) had spent five nights at Leidig's Hotel in Yosemite Valley. They had journeyed from Yosemite to Clark's Station (in the opposite direction that James would travel) over the twenty-four-mile South Fork Trail, Emerson digesting his breakfast pie.

———

"This is the dryest [sic] summer known in California for 30 years." James wrote Susan Goldmark from Yosemite. "All the waterfalls in the Valley but one are dry as a bone." That one was Vernal Fall, which James visited on horseback, a two and a half hour ride, almost two thousand feet above the valley floor. Forest fires, producing "acrid pungent smoke," inhibited distant views and caused them to seek higher ground. (8:412)

Our camping trip has been a great success

On the first day of a camping trip, 18 August 1898, William James and his party traveled from Yosemite to "Lake Tenago [Tenaya; 8,149 feet]—3 hours on foot & 5 on muleback." The men had four mules and a guide, John Sax. That night, sleeping at this 8,000-foot altitude palpitated James's heart—enough so for the party to change its original destination—the 12,590-foot top of Mount Conness, with its Conness glacier, six direct miles north of Tuolumne Meadows.[10] (8:415, 617)

On Day 2, 19 August, James rode 24 miles on horseback. He had traded his borrowed mule for one owned by the outfit's proprietor who, conveniently, was camped with his family at Lake Tenaya, too. Lunch at Soda Springs. Afternoon ride over a "wonderful pass to another little nameless lake," identified as Tioga Pass (9,945 feet) and Tioga Lake.[11]

On Day 3, 20 August, James recorded: "only eight miles to a pasture ground in the woods under Cloud's rest mountain [9,926 feet], where we stayed loafing and reading."

On Day 4, 21 August, James went "up Cloud's rest" in the morning. He stopped a few feet short of summit due to "my ridiculous fear on heights." The afternoon they stayed put, again "loafing."

On Day 5, 22 August, James and party returned to Wawona "by the rim of the Valley, Nevada falls & Glacier point, 12 miles riding, 10 walking, and 10 staging. The whole thing very grand and simple."

The next morning at Wawona, James conveyed both his itinerary and his impressions of the Sierra Nevada to his wife by mail:

"Seen from afar, from the lofty viewpoints, these Sierras form an awful wilderness of desolation of whitish granite mounds and peaks and precipices. But the ghastly pale gray surface is laced all over by thin lines of green following its crevices declivities and hollows, and inside these lines, when you get at them there is every sort of soft sylvan beauty, and through them innumerable lines of travel are made possible from one part of the scene to another. Immense pines, Lakelets, brooks, springs, meadows, rock-ledges, all sorts of beauties, a perfect feast for the artist at every turn. And almost everywhere the strange *nobility* that comes from smooth and simple lines, majestic size of elements, and vacant space between them. At every turn a kodak or water-colour subject; so that one could cry almost at not being an artist, and I *do* cry at having no "storage" for it all in the way of visual memory, only abstract ideas of what it was—so different from all that you find in the white mountains or the adirondacks, where the artist can hardly find a subject." (8:415)

Thus James described his first encounter with the Sierra Nevada to Alice. This is the most expansive landscape expression in his correspondence. Here James, who had seriously considered art as a career, despite his father's objections, became an artist in words. Or as Mark Twain put it when living in the Monadnock region of New

Hampshire: "Any place that is good for an artist in paint is good for an artist in morals and ink."[12]

Many artists also found subjects aplenty in the northeastern mountains of nineteenth-century America. One in fact resided at Wawona. English-born Thomas Hill, who turned sixty-nine in September 1898, had painted both the Sierra Nevada and the White Mountains, though primarily the former. He had traveled to the White Mountains in 1892 with his brother Edward, whose life was devoted to painting the White Mountains. Thomas Hill's daughter Estella Louise married Wawona proprietor John Washburn on 28 April 1885 in Oakland. They had one son, Clarence Arthur, on 18 January 1886. That same year a handsome studio was built for Hill at Wawona, where tourists sought and bought his art. In August 1896 he suffered a stroke. Though he kept working until his death in 1908, his output diminished. Doubtless, James knew his reputation, if not the man himself, whom he may have met at Wawona or in Hill's Cambridge, Massachusetts, studio in 1870-1871.[13]

———

Had John Muir, not John Sax, been James's Sierra Nevada guide, no doubt, Muir's "sermons" of "stones, storms, trees, flowers, and animals brimful of humanity" would have intrigued James. These subjects Muir covered in a series of articles in *The Atlantic Monthly* : November 1898, animals; December, birds; August 1899, Yosemite National Park; April 1900, forests of Yosemite, where for the first time Muir described in print his meeting with Emerson. He had not written about this until then for "Emerson had *forced* him to do all the talking," Muir told a *Century*

Magazine editor Robert Underwood Johnson, according to historian Stephen Fox. The April 1900 issue also contained Henry James's short story "Maud-Evelyn," which Alice read aloud to William, but apparently she did not read him Muir's essay. (3:114, 118) In August 1900, *The Atlantic Monthly* published Muir's "The Wild Gardens of Yosemite Park." It is likely that James saw, if not skimmed, Muir's essays. *The Atlantic Monthly*, an outstanding magazine, also featured William James's "Talks to Teachers on Psychology" in its February through May 1899 issues, as well as other works by his brother Henry and nature writers whom appealed to James, such as Thoreau, Sarah Orne Jewett, Olive Thorne Miller, Theodore Roosevelt, and Bradford Torrey, whose "Thoreau's Attitude Toward Nature," was in the November 1899 issue.[14]

———

James returned to Berkeley by 25 August 1898. The next night he lectured to 800 to 1,000 people gathered in the gymnasium at the University of California, Berkeley, by the Philosophical Union. James stayed with the Howisons, George and Lois. On Saturday, the 27th, he went to San Francisco to buy a hat.

———

Eight years later, in January 1906, James would cross the continent again, to California. This time he came to teach psychology at the then fifteen-year-old Stanford University (1891) for the spring semester. On 10 January he met his first class of two hundred regularly enrolled students. Six days later there were 300 enrolled. (11:143, 145) Alice joined him in February, nine days after her fifty-seventh birthday. Her husband could not meet her at San Francisco's station, nor walk any of the city's hills, for gout in both feet had left him hobbling about on crutches. While living with William on campus, Alice located the place of her father's former ranch in Mountain View, for which William had looked in vain a decade earlier. (8:428) The morning of 18 April the now legendary San Francisco earthquake rolled them out of bed. It decimated San Francisco and terminated Stanford's term for all faculty and students. The Jameses began their journey home, the "beautiful morning" of 26 April 1906. Friends drove them from Palo Alto to Oakland, over "this old country road we took with father fifty years ago," Alice wrote in her diary that night. The next day they ferried to San Francisco and from there boarded a Pullman car on the Southern Pacific eastbound.[15]

MOUNT MARCY REDUX

❧

1899

"In the woods one is morally safe. They do one's spirit a curious kind of good."
—*William James to his wife, 19 June 1899*

On the cusp of the 1899 summer solstice, William James, inveterate climber, fit and trim at fifty-seven, entered Adirondack Lodge on Heart Lake, nine miles south of the village of Lake Placid, New York.

Immediately upon arrival, that 17 June, James ascended nearby Mount Jo (2,876 feet), as he had done the previous year. Moving his lowermost foot forward first, he raised himself on the short, steep trail.[1] In less than a mile he had climbed 710 feet above Heart Lake to "one of the best views for the least effort in the Adirondacks," according to a modern guide book.[2]

James embraced the "freshness, the beauty, the stillness, the sacredness!" of the place. "The sweet cleanliness of the house." (8:552) The Lodge, however, then just nineteen years old, was deteriorating. The rotting logs of the foundation caused sagging floors and cracking walls, James observed. (8:557)

Sadly, too, the forest had been abused. The next day, 18 June, James walked "very slowly" southwestward to Indian Pass (2,834 feet), where he had stood some twenty-two years earlier, in August 1877. The first four or more miles of the total six miles (one way) were ruined, he wrote Alice, "by the ravages of lumbermen who are in there on a great scale, and now preparing for a still more serious onslaught next winter." He lamented the devestating impact on landscape and on those who came to be part of it. (8:553-554)

The day after his long walk, James read and took a nap at the lodge before visiting Van Hoevenburg, now manager of the Lake Placid Club. James "felt for the first time that good old solid elastic internal tone or returned wohlsein [good health, well-being]." (8:555)

After a rest day he walked for seven hours to and from Lake Colden (2,764 feet) via Avalanche Pass and Lake (2,863 feet), a total of ten miles. "Very beautiful in spite of clouds and an occasional drizzle—the sun came out well in the afternoon." The most challenging part of this journey was rounding the east side of Avalanche Lake, beset with boulders from sheer walls of 4,714-foot Mt. Colden. "The air here is unspeakably delicious." A "rainy, reading day" followed. (8:556-557).

Then came 22 June. James aspired to the acme of New York: Mt. Marcy (5,344 feet), whose summit he had reached only a year earlier. He made it up Marcy all right, solo. But, instead of returning to the lodge the way he had come, he somehow became disoriented and went in the opposite direction, east to Keene Valley, a challenging trek of nine miles. "[N]one the worse for it," he wrote Alice on 23 June. Then he traveled back to Cambridge, arriving on 27 June. (8:635) And in July he and Alice would be underway to Europe.

Over the summer, James would reveal more of what happened on Mt. Marcy. To his sons, on 10 July, he wrote: "I am tired, having done myself no good in getting lost on Marcy." (9:4) To brother Henry, on 8 August, he disclosed: "got lost . . . and converted what was to have been a 'walk' into a 13-hours scramble without food and with anxiety." (3:76-77) Four days later, on 12 August, he wrote Pauline Goldmark, his friend and climbing companion, that instead of a three-hour "downward saunter" northwest to the lodge, he had endured a seven-hour, nine-mile "scramble" through Johns Brook Valley to Keene Valley, arriving at 10:15 P.M. "This did me no good—quite the contrary, so I have come to Nauheim just in time." (9:22)

Bad Nauheim, a German spa, specialized in treatment of cardiac ailments. James's second Mt. Marcy traverse had exacerbated his heart condition— dilatation and chest-symptoms detected in autumn 1898, following his two-day "biggest tramp." Suffering from both overwork and the strain of the Mt. Marcy ordeals, James had come here to heal his heart and spirit.

After six weeks of the Nauheim regime of baths, relaxation, and strolls, in late August James confided to Carl Stumpf, a German psychologist, that "my mountain climbing days (such as they were) are over." (9:34)

PART THREE

The Post Mount Marcy Years

❧

1899–1910

Affliction would not be appeased
—Emily Dickinson, *Poems*

Were William James's climbing days over? Not completely. But Mount Marcy proved to be James's last great ascent. He would never be restored to the mountain climber he was before his ordeal with Mount Marcy. Try as he did to heal himself, in this last decade of his life, his ailments could not be remedied.

While not assaying the higher summits, James still embraced the mountains. His need for connection to the mountains persisted. He continued to draw strength from them, primarily the White Mountains and Adirondacks.

Here he absorbed their energy and beauty and calmness. He appreciated their presences all the more. They continued to restore his soul, if not his heart.

His delight in simply walking increased. He exulted in the hills he could negotiate. The one mountain that we know he climbed in this period was Skatutakee in southwestern New Hampshire. It offered him a slight elevation gain of 600 feet (as compared to nearby Monadnock's, of 1,500 to 1,700 feet, depending on trail, and Mt. Jo's, of 710 feet). Perhaps there were others. Yet his pleasure in this pursuit could not be measured.

1899–1901

to renew that dorsal contact to my native turf from which two years have separated me

Alice and William James left Cambridge on 15 July 1899 and did not return until 9 September 1901. While abroad their focus was on his healing: numerous tours at Bad-Nauheim, countless baths, doctor consults, Roberts-Hawley animal lymph injections. Yet, William and Alice tired of hotel life and longed for home. James was not able to walk much: "the least exertion pains and tires me," he wrote from Rome in mid-December 1900 in a letter to Boston banker Henry Lee Higginson. (9:383) He pecked away at his Gifford Lectures, which he delivered between 16 May and 17 June 1901. His nervous condition improved and regressed. Through all this he sustained his reading and his writing of letters to family and friends. "I find letters a great thing to keep one from slipping out of life." (9:540) His spirit kept him alive.

On 13 August 1901, before returning home, James contemplated a restorative mountain sojourn. The Vosges in northeastern France won over the Harz in Germany. The former, a relatively low mountain range, attained its highest elevation in Grand Ballon at 4,672 feet, being not as high as Marcy in New York nor as low as Mansfield in Vermont. James planned to spend a week, "a nachcur" (rest after treatment; James meant kur, not cur) in "the higher air." However, when he and Alice arrived on 12 August, no hotel rooms were available. Thus, they proceeded to Henry's Lamb House in Rye, and sailed home on the last day of August. (9:530-531, 635)

No sooner had they set foot in Cambridge than William, afflicted with acute "nervous prostration," left for Chocorua, on 11 September. Their home being rented, he stayed with the Salters at Hill Top "to renew that dorsal contact to my native turf from which two years have separated me, and without which I verily believe I never can get well." The next morning he ascended the ledge "without difficulty. . . and spent the forenoon there." Gradually, he adjusted to the White Mountain landscape. At first it felt impoverished compared to all he had seen abroad, the piece de resistance being Switzerland. His letters caution about mixing hemispheres. When the Salters left, he spent three days with the Merrimans at Stonehurst, returning to Cambridge the last day of September. (9:537, 538)

At the close of 1901, James declared himself "now vastly better than at any time in the two years past." (9:565) Though he had not been to the Adirondacks since June 1899, he felt that his experience of mountain climbing there was the greatest influence in his life. (9:243) *divinity of air and light and water*

On 1 April 1902 William and Alice again sailed to the British Isles. Between 13 May and 9 June, James gave his second round of Gifford lectures at Edinburgh; these were published the month he finished as *The Varieties of Religious Experience*, now a classic. The next day, 10 June, William and Alice began their transatlantic voyage home, arriving in Boston on 19 June. (3:206)

Two days later James traveled to Chocorua "to get nervously well." (10:65) From there on 2 July he wrote letters to Sarah Wyman Whitman and to brother Henry. To Sarah, he lamented: "the whole country getting overgrown with scurvy bush, and not a decent tree or field anywhere visible." Yet despite the devastation of clear-cutting in the northern forest, James found "the freedom to range over it and use it all, the emergence from one's bed room right on to the face of it, the transparence and fragrance and divinity of air and light and water, the spirituality & Americanity just nourish one's very soul." (10:75) And to Henry: "if one can't recover health in these conditions, then no conditions anywhere will restore it." (3:207)

James made short trips to the Merrimans at Stonehurst in Intervale. There on 1 August he had "a panoramic view of the White Mountains," except Mount Washington "hid in filmy mist." (10:97) He returned to Stonehurst on 18 September for twenty-four hours. From there he wrote Sarah Wyman Whitman, whom he had visited in August at her Beverly Farms home, The Old Place, for a day and two nights. He told her that it was "just as well" she could not come north, for he wanted her "to do it in the freshness of the springtide of the soul," when he could "play the part of host with success." He lamented having suffered "Too much activity, I think, too much sociability." He observed: "I have enjoyed walking and scrambling in the woods much as of yore," As in Septembers past, he reminded her and himself, "I must get off now, to be alone in the mountains for a week ere we return." (10:104,128)

At the end of August, he informed Grace Norton: "I *walk* somewhat as in old times . . . The country seems as beautiful as ever—it is good that when age takes away the zest from so many things, it seems to make no difference at all in one's capacity for enjoying landscape and the aspects of Nature." (10:115)

He did not go to Keene Valley. A painful decision for him, yet "the prudent one to make," he concluded. Returning to Cambridge on 3 October, he took up his "moderate lecturing duties. " (10:132-133)

1903

So keep growing intimate.

—*William James to son Aleck,* 29 March 1903

From 28 March to 9 April 1903, James became more intimate with the Asheville, North Carolina, landscape. James spent the afternoon of 28 March riding the trolly and walking about Asheville. The "country is simply lovely, and the air delicious," he wrote to Alice that night. (10:221) He had regained his health following ten days of "extreme pressure, intellectual and social." "The thing that appears to break me up more than anything else is too much society."

The next day a flock of gray buntings graced his morning walk. In the afternoon a "North Easter" put snow on the hills. "I am feeling extraordinarily well," he told Alice. "The altitude has something to do with it." (10:222) Asheville sits at 2,100 feet. His primary residence was the Victoria Inn, to which he moved, from the more-expensive Kenilworth Inn. Twice he dined with George and Edith Vanderbilt at their Biltmore estate, through which he was driven—for two and a half hours on the afternoon of 2 April. (10:224, 227) "Vanderbilt owns a strip of land 50 miles long by 15 broad," James wrote to Henry. He "is doing every kind of work, forestry nursery, dairy, horticulture, stock raising, road perfecting, and is a model to the rich men all through the country." (3:228-229

The Biltmore House, of Richard Morris Hunt design, is a French Renaissance Revival château, according to architectural historian Martin Filler. It "is still the largest private residence in America." James did approve of Hunt's architecture, however. (3:229, 10:601) Frederick Law Olmsted convinced Vanderbilt to reject the "empty ostentation of the Gilded Age" and "turn the surrounding land into a model of modern sustainable forestry."[1]

On Sunday 5 April, James made a twenty-four-mile excursion to the Esmeralda Inn for a night and forenoon. With the inn's "scotch yankee" landlord, they crossed the Broad River and "went some distance up a trail on the hill side before dark." The next morning's "scramble up a brook to a high waterfall," reminded James of Keene Valley. (10:229-230)

"It is a sweet spot," he wrote to his daughter Peggy, summing up his impression of the Asheville area, "but too artificially civilized in the immediate Biltmore neighborhood." (10:230)

Again the "open air life" banished his excessive fatigue. "[T]hough all my walking has to be slow," he wrote Henry on 7 April from the Victoria. "Yesterday I had a half hour's scramble up a very steep and slippery mountain brook and essuyé-d [suffered] no bad effects whatever. This is great, compared with two years ago." (3:228)

All the while James kept an eye out for a possible North Carolina summer home for the family, but this never came to be. This was his last trip to Asheville, North Carolina.

1891

An earlier Asheville sojourn

James's spring 1903 trip to Asheville contrasts with his first visit there in summer 1891. Then James, aged forty-nine, had climbed three major mountains of the Southern Appalachians, including its highest, Mount Mitchell (6,684 feet) on 18-19 August. He had entrained to the Roan Mountain Station Hotel at 2,600 feet on the North Carolina-Tennessee border. From there on Saturday, 22 August he had surmounted Roan (6,285 feet), sleeping atop in the Cloudland Hotel of which only a historic marker remains. A two-mule stage carried him down on Sunday afternoon "in a shower of rain." (7:192-193) By train he had continued east to Cranberry, North Carolina, and by stage to Linville for the night at the Eseeola Inn. On Monday, 24 August, he had climbed Grandfather Mountain (5,964 feet).

Again, all this was "strictly necessary for health," he had written to Alice before heading north. (7:186) From Chocorua, in the end of August, he took time to write an enthusiastic essay about his journey, which appeared in the *New York Evening Post*, 3 September 1891. "The walk up Mitchell's peak is the most beautiful forest walk (only five hours) I ever made," he recalled.[2]

1894

I never breathed such sweet air.

Three years later, on 13 June 1894, James had returned to North Carolina with Charles F. Atkinson, a Boston businessman. The then new hotel in Blowing Rock (which is no more) at 4,000 feet in the Blue Ridge Mountains nicely accommodated them. The men spent Friday morning the 15th on "one high hilltop with our books." Despite a month's draught that covered the landscape with "powdery dust," "an untimely hard frost two weeks ago", and oppressive heat, James was glad to be there for its "complete change." On 17 June James and Atkinson moved west to Linville, where the "blight of the trees" was not evident. That day and the next they walked on the road "6 or 8" miles. On Friday 22 June James made his second ascent of Grandfather Mountain (the first was in 1891). The next day at six in the morning he had an "entrancing walk" of five miles on a forest road—"I never breathed such sweet air." James and Atkinson left at seven to begin the thirty-six-hour trip home. (7:516-520)

1904

Henry James at Chocorua

The big event of the year was the arrival of brother Henry at Chocorua on 2 September 1904. He stayed for a fortnight. William had done enough writing for the summer. He was "going to take a complete rest for September," he wrote to Pauline Goldmark on 3 September. "The prospect of walking a good deal pleases me greatly." (10:460,464) And walk William and Henry did. "[U]nder the consummate art of autumn," Henry wrote in *The American Scene,* they trod the local turf. On their one excursion Henry did climb an unidentified "hill," overlooking the village of Jackson. (10: 474) Evidently, the "silvered summit" of Chocorua with "the *allure* of a minor Matterhorn" was not reached. (AS: 368, 372-373)

After the brothers parted on the morning of 21 September, William "trudged across lots to our hill top," and lay there with his "back against a stone, scribbling . . . these lines" to Pauline Goldmark. In a letter to Alice on 22 September, he wrote of the prior day's "open air" morning tramp to what he now called "Gibbens hill top," in honor of her family. The next day, the 23rd, William woke at 3.30 A.M. At 24° "too cold to get to sleep again," he took a "*beautiful* & exhilarating walk" to the village to mail Alice's letter—"the whole land white, road & all, with frost, & a beautiful fog on the lake." The 24th was the only all-day rain of the season, and the clear sky that night presented "the most delicate pageant of soft clouds & vapor mingling with the endless refinement of the foliage." James finished reading Hector Berlioz's memoirs. (10: 475-478, 480)

William returned to Cambridge for the start of school on Thursday, 29 September; he delivered his first lecture to students in his and Royce's Philosophy 9: Metaphysics on Saturday 1 October. On 7 October he addressed the International Peace Conference meeting in Cambridge.

1905

Greece is really Alpine country

On 11 March 1905, William James left for Italy and Greece, not returning for three months, until 11 June. His purpose was to attend the fifth International Congress of Psychology in Rome, at the end of April.

First came Greece, where James arrived by steamer from Marseilles on 3 April. His appreciation of Athens, "a delectable little place," was not without a longing for Chocorua. On 7 April he went from Athens by carriage seven miles southwest to the port of Pireaus. Aboard a steamer in the Gulf of Corinth, he saw snow-capped mountains along the Peloponnese peninsula to the west; "but the mountains on both shores entirely uninhabited." The next morning he traveled two-and-a-half hours by carriage from Itéa (James's Etria) up the "beautifully gentle zigzag gradients of the national road" to Delphi. At the start snowy Parnassus (8,060 feet) was visible for ten minutes. Returning to Athens by boat from Itéa at five o'clock on 9 April, William wrote Alice of his excursion, concluding, "Greece is really Alpine country."(11: 3-6)

On 16 April James left Athens for Mycenae, which figures prominently in Homer's *Iliad*. Of the journey, he commented: "in point of weather, landscape, and ancient remains, was one of the most impressive days I ever lived through." "The country all day long was perfectly ravishing . . . and the early effects of light on the earth and sea and mountains for an hour after leaving Athens were exquisite. Then came barren limestone hills through which the train wound slowly till after some 6 hours it reached Mycenae Station." There James and Scottish philosopher James Seth sauntered about the town "and part way up the peak." (11:10) By train from Corinth the "road ran close to the shore of the Gulf of Corinth, through Patras, and was beautiful beyond comparison. Blue water, Mountains over the bay, sprouting vineyards, and olives in the fore ground, peasants ad libitum, all of them artists models, of whatever age." He reached Olympia "in the magic of the moonlight at 9." Being in Olympia country appealed to him greatly. It reminded him of Vermont: "low hills all round, verdure-clad, sweet, and homelike & cheerful." (11:11-12) Greece's acme, Mt. Olympus at 9,570 feet, James did not mention. He regretted having spent so much time in Athens, which left him only the next morning to enjoy the Olympia countryside, for he was back in Patras by early afternoon.

Flagstones, Hancock, NewHampshire

On late Friday morning, 8 September 1905, William James took a short train ride from Cambridge to Hancock, a small village of 640 residents in southwestern New Hampshire. From the depot (now a museum), horse and carriage transported him two miles to Hunts Pond (1,296 feet) and another mile-and-a-half south to Kings Highway.

Here his dear friend from Newport days, Thomas Sergeant Perry, now sixty, and his junior by three years, Lilla Cabot Perry, were concluding their second summer. On 9 April they had celebrated their thirty-first wedding anniversary. In 1903, Lilla Perry had bought this late eighteenth-century farmhouse with 250 acres. Her husband, according to his biographer, Virginia Harlow, "agreed to the purchase on condition that he should not have to go and look at it."[1] When not there the Perrys resided at 312 Marlborough Street, Boston.

The farmhouse, at 34 Kings Highway, Hancock, with additions and alterations, is still serving the Perry family. A 1900 photograph of the structure, known as the Tuttle House of 1786, for its original owners, was shown to me by the current owners, Peter and Pam Moffat. It reveals a three-story, weathered, wood-sided, single-chimney Federal, with pointed pediment over the entrance facing the lane.[2] This gives a sense of the Perry cottage at the time of William James's visit. I later learned from Pam Moffat that Henry James came here, too,—evidently, five years later—in 1910—and is credited with christening the farm Flagstones.[3]

The "highway," still single-lane, is edged with a low, stone wall in front of the house, and is paved for the downhill section past the house, To the right of the entrance stand a great gingko and a Chinese or Persian lilac—the latter with "an unbelievably fragrant flowering," the Moffats exclaim, "but only every other year!" The gingko and lilac tower over the roof. Hardly a car passes while I am there. Stillness and solitude surround the place.

We walk through the living room and a mini-library which now joins a former shed to the south end of the house. The "shed" has abundant natural light.Peter's desk is below the east-facing windows, which look out over the road. A sofa stands in front of a north-end fireplace; the long side of a Chickering piano lines the room's west wall. Lilla Cabot's paintings—one, a Monadnock snow scene—complete the decor. Sitting on a small screened porch off the "shed," I learn about Pam and Peter.

They met in Cambridge in 1952, he Harvard Class of 1952; she, Radcliffe, 1956-*ex*. She left college to marry him on 28 December 1953 in Washington, DC. (She later graduated from American University.) Lilla Cabot and Thomas Sergeant Perry are Peter's great grandparents; Alice Perry and Joseph Grew, his grandparents, and Lilla Cabot Grew and Jay Pierrepont Moffat, his parents. Pam and Peter have three children: Sarah, Matthew and Nathaniel. Peter's association with Flagstones began with his birth in 1932. "It was always the ultimate home during my father's and my own foreign service years."

Back to James's 1905 visit. On Saturday, 9 September, James walked up hill with Lilla and Thomas Perry's three daughters, Margaret, twenty-nine, Edith, twenty-six, and Alice, twenty-one. They appear in their mother's portraits. *TheTrio* (c.1898-1900), for example, shows them playing cello, violin, piano.[4] The young women performed "impromptu musicales," according to Peter Moffat.

Less than a month after William James's visit, on 7 October 1905, Alice, the youngest Perry daughter, would be the first to wed. Her husband-to-be Joseph Clark Grew, Harvard 1902, was likely known to James; he had joined the US Foreign Service a year earlier, in 1904. Their marriage produced Lilla Cabot Grew, on 30 November 1907, who, on 27 July 1927, married Jay Pierrepont Moffat.[5]

Though James did not identify their hill climb, it was surely Skatutakee Mountain (2,002 feet), which rose some 660 feet from the farm's west side, through what was then a rock-walled pasture, not today's mixed forest of birch and pine. A stroll of a mile-and-a-half put them atop with a splendid view of Monadnock to the south.

Thanks to Eleanor Briggs and Meade Cadot, Skatutakee is now part of the Harris Center's Supersanctuary, a land trust of some twenty-one thousand acres. Eleanor Briggs's grandfather, and then her father owned Skatutakee. Meade Cadot, as director of the Harris Center for thirty-three years (1975-2008), kept promoting land acquisitions and conservation easements. When I last checked with him, in fall 2014, he reported "well over 700 acres added to the Supersanctuary arena this past year. More on the way."[6]

When James visited the Perrys in 1905, Thomas was engaged in finishing a short, 100-page, biography of historian-philosopher John Fiske (1842-1901) to be published the following year. Perry credited James for his encouragement.[7] (11:94, 571)

The Perrys were preparing to return to Paris, where they had lived before, and to spend three more summers at Giverny with Claude Monet. Though Monet did not teach students, Lilla so admired him and his art that they became close friends. In those halcyon days, Monet, whom she saw paint only once indoors, encouraged her painting of landscapes in the open air; she also did outdoor figures. When not painting, she gayly bicycled the streets. The Perrys' 1909 summer with Monet in Giverny was their last; they left France that year never to return. When the Moffats visited Monet's Giverny, they were surprised to find one of Lilla Cabot Perry's paintings in the master's bedroom.

The Moffats own about twenty-five acres, surrounding their house. Two plump wild turkeys grazed their mowed meadow on the other side of a dry brook. When I visited, during the summer 2010 draught, Peter observed: "There's not a mosquito in New Hampshire." The Moffats have seen bear, deer, and bobcats. No moose, however, though they are in town. Loons pass over Flagstones on their four-mile arc due south from Willard Pond to Juggernaut Pond. On my way here, out of the far side of a perfectly quiet Hunts Pond, a loon's hallowed call startled me.

Down beyond where turkeys peck sits Lilla's former studio, its north window boarded. For Lilla, as her work attests, this was a painter's paradise. Her last exhibited painting, at the Guild of Boston Artists, *Mist on the Mountain*, an oil of 1931, blended Monadnock with sky/atmosphere so as to remove distinctions and make the two one.[8]

Before James returned to Cambridge on Monday afternoon, 11 September, he walked to Juggernaut Pond. Nestled on the southeast side of Skatutakee, not far from the Perry place, this spring-fed reservoir now provides Hancock's water supply, though the Moffats rely on their own well. Peter praised this pond as the state's most beautiful. We would walk there another day.

1906

My hill climbing activities are curtailed

On 3 May 1906 William and Alice James arrived in Boston from California.

On 6 June William boarded the train for Chocorua. "I seemed to enjoy every foot of the way hither—the vegetation was so wild & green & fresh that my whole being greeted it," he wrote Alice the next day from the Chocorua Hotel. "Arrived in pouring rain." Though he had recently expressed, "My hill climbing activities are curtailed," he walked "over the hill" to the nearby Salter's home and back on the 10 , and the next day he walked for three hours around the lake. (These distances he estimated at five and three miles respectively.) Pain in his knee forced James to return to Cambridge on 14th. (11:232,:228, 235, 589)

James's letters and diary track his travels:

23 July to 1 August, visit Charles and Grace Eliot at Southwest Harbor, Mount Desert, Maine. (11:252)

8 to 12 August, visit Sophia Shaler in North Tisbury, Martha's Vineyard (DWJ). Her husband, Nathaniel Southgate Shaler, had died four months earlier, on 10 April.

16 to 22 August, Maine coast again: Rockland, Owl's Head, Swans Island, North Haven; steamer from Rockland to Portland to Boston.[1] (DWJ; 11:256)

On 25 August, James left for the Adirondacks. Even

knowing that this is the place "where I can't climb," he could "at least lie on the *ground*" and read. After a night at the Westport Inn, James arrived at Glenmore on East Hill at noon. Afflicted with an assortment of symptoms—"tightness of the head, incipient headache, running of the heart, and restlessness in bed"—James made the "painful decision" to leave, "probably never to return." "My relations with this region are at an end!" (11:259, 260-261).

On 29 August, James went south to Putnam Camp. Despite his past—"I always sleep poorly at the Shanty"—he slept well this time. (11:260) "This end of the Valley is after all vastly more wonderful than the other," he wrote Alice on 30 August. (11:263) "It is four years since I've been here," he wrote daughter Margaret Mary (called Peggy). (Actually, it had been seven years, since his 1899 mishap on Marcy that brought him to this end of the valley.) "[T]he kind and variety of beauty here is incomparable & unique . . . Never was so *romantic* a place, with its varied windings,—always a new mountain peering over a new sylvan mystery, and the shafts of the sun always changing their direction . . ." He did not think Peggy's brothers "sufficiently alive to the beauties of this place, but, I rejoice, dear Peggy, that you are." (11:264) Ten days later he wrote Peggy again, happy that she shared his feelings for Keene Valley. "I want never to be cut off from it . . . I should like my children to keep up some connexion [sic] with it forever. . . I shall sell the East Hill land at the first opportunity." (11:266). On 4 September James made a solo climb to Mosso's ledge.* That he could do such things again lifted his spirits.[2] (11:594) The next day he left for Lake George and then Chocorua, where he stayed from 10 to 27 September.

*Named for Angelo Mosso (1846-1910), Italian physiologist.

1907

in my beloved & exquisite Keene Valley

William James returned to his "beloved & exquisite Keene Valley" for the first three weeks of September 1907. "I am very glad to be up her again," he wrote Henry, "free from all suggestion of any of my responsibilities. Nothing rests one like that. In spite of rainy weather the valley is supremely beautiful still." Here he was "able to do a good deal of uphill walking"— his first since the Mt. Marcy incident of 1899—"with good rather than bad effects, much to my joy."

After they closed the Chocorua House for the winter, Alice left for Cambridge and William, for Stonehurst, in Intervale, New Hampshire. He stayed with the Bryces, who "had taken the Merriman's House for the summer." Now the woods are "beginning to redden beautifully. With the sun behind them some maples look like stained glass windows," William wrote Henry. On 5 October William "took a 3 hours walk here, 3/4 of an hour of it up hill. I have to go alone, and slowly; but its none the worse for that and makes me feel like old times." (3: 343, 345)

1908

real natural relations with the country

In late May and early June 1908, William gave the Hibbert Lectures at Manchester College, Oxford, England. Afterwards he and Alice stayed in England and Europe for five months, not returning home until Friday 16 October.

The next day, James departed for New Hampshire. He explained why in a letter to his son Alexander James, who was studying with a tutor in Oxford: "I want to have, before the winter sets in, at least a week of what I call real natural relations with the country, lying down on mother earth, and going into woods. Not an hour of that did I have this summer." (12:106)

Even England's glorious Lake District—nestled in the Cumbrian Mountains of which Scafold Peak (3,210 feet) is the highest—had not fulfilled James's need for "real natural relations." Lodging at Oak Bank in Grasmere (24 June to 2 July 1908), he found automobiles, and "tourist conveyances of every description crowding the splendid macadamized roads, and keeping one from sitting down anywhere." To fellow philosopher-psychologist Charles Augustus Strong James wrote on 28 June: "*This* country is splendid if one have proper legs and wind, which I haven't." (12:37-38) Mostly, his touring consisted of riding about in stage coaches, through the treeless hills, which offered no shade, he wrote Pauline Goldmark. "It is a lovely country, however, for pedestrianizing in cooler weather. Mountains and valley compressed together as in the Adirondacks, great reaches of pink and green hillside and lovely lakes, the higher parts quite fully alpine in character but for the fact that no snow mountains form the distant background." (12:43)

On his last day in Grasmere, on 1 July, James visited Dove Cottage (now open to the public) near the east shore of Grasmere Lake, where William Wordsworth and his sister Dorothy had resided a century earlier, from 1799 to 1808. Had he relished William Wordsworth's *A Guide Through the District of the Lakes* (1835)?[1] Here the poet's love of the landscape is ever apparent. Each valley distinctive. Of all the lakes, Windermere held "so many fresh beauties," due to its size, ten miles long, its islands, and "*two* vales at the head, with their accompanying mountains of nearly equal dignity." (5) Also evident here is Wordsworth's conservation ethic, his concern for the environment. Wordsworth paid attention to the flora, objecting to the planting of large tracts of larch in "lovely vales," wishing to confine them to "barren and exposed ground," as in Scotland. (82) Above all he wanted the scenery protected for its many gifts, among them beauty, serenity, repose. He saw the Lakes as a national treasure, in which everyone has "a right and interest who has an eye to perceive and a heart to enjoy." (92) The Wordsworths would be gratified to know that their Lakeland was made a national park in 1951.

"James had read all of Wordsworth," philosopher John Elof Boodin remembered. Wordsworth's "purity of style and intimacy with nature" appealed to James, who sprinkled his own work with quotations from the great Romantic poet. James considered Wordsworth and Dante believers, like himself, in "an eternal moral order," from which derives the "extraordinary tonic and consoling power of their verse." They both acknowledged the healing spirit of nature.[2]

After Wordsworth, Ruskin. James took a stage ten miles southwest to Coniston and two-and-a-half miles farther along the northeast shore of Coniston Water to Brantwood, where John Ruskin had lived from September 1872 until his death in January 1900. Paying a penny to enter the Ruskin Museum, James was moved to see the critic's "busy handiwork, exquisite & loving, in the way of drawing, sketching, engraving & note-taking, and also such a lot of fotografs of him especially in his old age."[3] (12:48) At the lake's head stood the Old Man of Coniston, rising to 2,635 feet; James did not climb it. Did it recall to him the Old Man of the Mountain at Franconia Notch in the White Mountains of New Hampshire? James returned to Oak Bank, half by coach, then five miles by foot. (12:41).

The next day, 2 July, Oak Bank was too hot and crowded for him; James departed. He did not go far. He traveled about eight miles northeast by stage to the village of Patterdale; there he lodged at the Ullswater Hotel at the south end of the seven-mile-long Ullswater Lake, which, he wrote, "*much* resembles Lake George." (12:44) How he must have missed not making the acquaintance of Helvellyn (3,118 feet), the Lakeland's most tramped summit. Instead, on the afternoon of 4 July, he joined new English friends, the Squances, on a forty-mile automobile tour of the country: Keswick, Grasmere, Ambleside. (12:47) "I am walking here a couple of hours daily, cool and inclined to mist and drizzle, but very fine scenery," he wrote Alice. (12:50) He left Patterdale and the Lake District on 9 July for London.

The Tale of Jemima Puddle-Duck

Between Coniston and Windermere east of the village of Near Sawrey on the west side of Windermere Lake stands Hill Top. Beatrix Potter acquired this farm at age thirty-nine in 1905 and completed renovating it by October 1907. She began to set her stories here. All James had to do was consult her *The Tale of Tom Kitten*, of September 1907, for scenes of the countryside, her gardens, which contained "something out of nearly every garden in the village"— such was the generosity of her community—and of her animals: Herdwick sheep, a collie, hens, cows, pigs, ducks. One of those ducks she drew in flight wearing bonnet and shawl; the duck soars over stone-walled pastures in search of a place to lay her eggs. *The Tale of Jemima Puddle-Duck*, appeared in July 1908, coinciding with James's England itinerary; this book, now a children's classic, shows Hill Top scenes, countryside, even the Tower Banks Arms in Near Sawrey, a pub with beer garden and three rooms owned now by the National Trust.

In September 1907, *The Tale of Tom Kitten* was published. It was dedicated to "all Pickles," which meant, according to biographer Linda Lear, "free-thinking, exuberant people." William James was an adult-version Pickle. Sadly, he and Potter never met. Beatrix was about her Sawrey fell farm that spring and summer, at least in March and August, and with her parents, who rented Stock Park,

Lake Side, Ulverston, for the end of July and first half of August, about ten miles south of Hill Top.

Though Beatrix lived with her parents in London, at 2 Bolton Gardens, until her marriage to William Heelis of Hawkeshead in 1913, she came to her fell farm whenever she could. She had a Lake District heart and soul. Over time she purchased some 4,000 acres of Lakeland and willed it to the National Trust.[4]

A founder of the National Trust, in 1895, was Hardwicke Drummond Rawnsley, priest of Crosthwaite Church, Keswick, since 1883. His devotion to the beauty of the lakes led him to found The Lake District Defense Society in 1883 in Wray. This devotion—shared by his mentor, John Ruskin, who wanted to protect his estate—was infectious and influenced Beatrix Potter, among others.

On 9 August 1906, the National Trust celebrated its acquisition of Gowbarrow Park, 750 acres "of woodland and heather fellside along the northwest shore of Ullswater." Some 1,600 people attended the event. Rawnsley, who had toured the nation speaking on behalf of the preservation of this land, attended as did his invited guest, Woodrow Wilson, the two having just met. Wilson, fifty-two, the then president of Princeton University, was making his fourth visit to the Lake District, the second with his wife and the first with their three daughters. Arriving 10 July 1906, the Wilsons rented Loughrigg Cottage in Rydal— "at the heart of the region we most love"—for almost three months. This was his longest stay. During that summer, besides Rawnsley, Wilson met local artist Fred Yates(1854-1919). They formed a lifelong friendship. Yates painted portraits of all five Wilsons; Princeton University displays one of Wilson.[5]

When Wilson first saw the Lake District, on 29 June 1896, it captured his heart. Wilson traveled southward by train from Carlisle, where his mother, Janet, had been born and his grandfather, Thomas Woodrow, had served as minister of the Annetwell Street Congregational Chapel—before family emigrated to the United States, in November 1835. Wilson's destination was Keswick. From there he bicycled "16 enchanting miles," he wrote his wife, Ellen, to Grasmere and Rydal, where he saw both Wordsworth residences.[6] (Rydal Cottage was rented then and not open to the public as it is now.)

Wilson returned to the Lake District for the summer of 1908, this time on his own. His arrival in Grasmere, on 15 July, six days after James's departure on 9 July, left no chance of their even being in the same place at the same time. Except for a three-day bicycle tour of the western lakes, and an August week with Andrew Carnegie at his Skibo home in Scotland, Wilson stayed at the Rothay Hotel in Grasmere, "free to enjoy the blessed peace and beauty of this dear land," he wrote Ellen. (*PWW* 18:393) Again, Wilson bicycled about at a moderate pace and walked up and down the hills; for instance, Shoulthwaite Fell. He also "took the only automobile ride I have ever enjoyed," he wrote Ellen, with the Marburgs of Baltimore and their coachman: "the lights on the hills, as the road turned first this way and then that amidst the shifting panorama of fields and fells, fairly took one's breath with a sort of rapture." (*PWW* 18:394) Staying much longer than James, Wilson did not begin his return to Glasgow for the boat to America until 2 September.[7]

This was Wilson's last vacation in the Lake District. Though he intended to return, he never did. The one exception was his "pilgrimage of the heart" to Carlisle at the close of 1918, following World War One. At the time, Wilson was serving his second term as president of the United States.

———

Back to William James: after "a pretty fatiguing voyage of head winds, and heavy seas," he and Alice arrived home from England, on 16 October 1908. The following morning James took the train to Silver Lake, New Hampshire. From there he traveled three miles north to Hill Top, the summer home of the Salters.[8]

He was just in time for an evening walk to Whitton's pond, which Salter Hill (1,140 feet) overlooked to north, "thru that mysterious back pasture road," he wrote Alice. He was happy to be there: "I never saw the country so sentimentally beautiful . . . The trees hold all their fire, gold, green, & scarlet. The air is smoke-hazed, there is no wind, no people, no sound." Two days later, "the horse being lame," James walked to their Chocorua Lake house, three miles east. "Your improvements are great," he commended his wife. (12:108,109) Yet, he lamented to Pauline Goldmark, "this indian summer weather, is just heart-breaking," a "pathetic scene of regret, morbid and weak." (12:110) Was he projecting his own unconscious feelings about his condition in the autumn of his life? While autumn lingered, the Salters stayed, and so did James, not returning to Cambridge until 4 November, except briefly, for the funeral of Charles Eliot Norton on 23 October.

living in a state of high contentment and communion with nature

"It hasn't gone well with my health this summer, and beyond a little reading, I have done no work at all," James wrote on 28 September 1909 to Swiss psychologist Theodore Flournoy. (12:333) His summer followed its usual flow pattern. The last week of May James was in the Berkshires, staying four nights in the Red Lion Inn (still open) in Stockbridge. From there he saw the landscape mostly by automobile, though he did report to Alice some painless walking. On 25 May, Katie Bullard drove him in her car northward to the Mount Lebanon Shaker village, New York, and the next day southeastward to Tyringham. On 27 May a Mrs. Haven drove him to Salisbury, Connecticut. (12:240-241; 614-615)

Five years earlier, in 1904, Edith Wharton had motored Henry James around her beloved Berkshires. And six years before that, at the end of October 1898, John Muir had made a short visit with the Gilders, Richard Watson and Helena de Kay, at their Four Brooks Farm in Tyringham.

The better part of June 1909, William James resided with his brother-in-law, William Salter, at Hill Top in Silver Lake, New Hampshire. Here he was "living in a state of high contentment and communion with nature," he wrote Pauline Goldmark. "I find that by walking slowly enough I can get about anywhere and everywhere I will." Inspecting the Salters' apple orchard, he found blossoms everywhere. (12:275, 259) He returned to Cambridge for Harvard's commencement on 30 June.

In early July William and Alice were busy opening their Chocorua home. The task of maintaining their "nestling hamlet" was beyond James's energy. Nor could labor be hired easily. Frustrated, James was of the mind to sell the place; however, Alice, who did most of the work, wanted to keep it.

The big change that summer was James's not going to Keene Valley. Ironically, that very summer, both Sigmund Freud and Carl Jung made it to Keene Valley. They had traveled to America to lecture at Clark University's Twentieth Anniversary Celebration at the invitation of its president G. Stanley Hall. Freud and Jung stayed at Hall's house on the Clark campus in Worcester, Massachusetts, from 6-10 September. James arrived in Worcester in the late afternoon of Thursday 9 September and overnighted at Hall's with his guests. The next morning at eleven in the art room atop the Clark Library, James listened to Freud's fourth lecture in a series of five, "On Psychoanalysis."[1] As Freud knew that James would be in the audience, he shifted his topic from infantile sexuality to dreams. He spoke in German. Later Freud walked James to the train, so that William could join Alice at Chocorua the next day. (12:320-321)

After the Clark conference, at the invitation of James Jackson Putnam, Freud and Jung arrived at Putnam Camp, Keene Valley, New York. They traveled there on 15 September via horse and carriage from Lake Placid, staying in a three-room cabin called the Chatterbox. "Everything is left very rough and primitive but it comes off," Freud wrote his family in Vienna. That afternoon Putnam lead them up the "nearest mountain." Though Freud's letter does not identify this mountain, it must have been the Giant (4,627 feet). Here Freud became "acquainted with the utter wildness of such an American landscape." The fifty-three-year-old Freud, who was nursing his "American colitis," admitted being "not equal" to the task.[2]

Fortunately for Freud the next day, the date of his letter home, was rainy. On 18 September, Freud and Jung departed for New York via Albany.[3] As for Dr. Putnam, Prochnik says, he and his family continued their yearly pilgrimage to the camp. In his seventies, he was still climbing the "exhausting peak" of the Giant.[4]

1910

Alice and William James spent half of 1910 abroad. James returned to Bad-Nauheim to strengthen his heart, with a bathing regimen. He had last spent time there in 1900. Now his walking was minimal. I am "in rather sorry plight with angina and dyspnoea," he wrote Thomas Sergeant Perry in late May, "but I hope the baths will check the nasty progress down-hill of the past year." Unfortunately, they did not.

On 23 June, William left Nauheim with Alice and Henry, beginning the long trip home. They passed through Switzerland and Paris before arriving in London by 13 June. (12:571) and onto Lamb House, Henry's home in Rye. The trio departed for London on 11 August, the date of William's last entry in his diary, and from there the next day to Liverpool where the Jameses boarded the *Empress of Britain,* arriving in Quebec on 18 August. The last part of William's final journey was by train southward through New England's northern forest and mountains to Chocorua. He wrote his last letter on 21 August and took his last breath of alpine air in Alice's arms mid-afternoon of 26 August. (12:574-575)

APPRECIATIONS

I am most grateful to all who have contributed to our understanding of William James, especially his biographers and his correspondence editors, Ignas K.Skrupskelis and Elizabeth M. Berkeley, with the assistance of Wilma Bradbeer, and the writers of the introductions to those superlative twelve volumes. Without their devoted scholarship and that of those listed in the notes and bibliography, this could not have been written.

Add to this, the gifted guidance of editor Susan Pollack, and publisher Dede Cummings, and those listed below, and you have a community endeavor. I am indebted to the insights and writings of Robert D. Richardson, Jr. and John Elder.

And what would I have done without:

John and Mary Carnahan, Joann Nichols, Brattleboro Historical Society.

Elizabeth Hall, Professor of Art, Stockton College, New Jersey.

Jocelyn Hebert, editor, *Long Trail News,* Green Mountains Club, Vermont,

Archie Hobson and his most valuable *The Cambridge Gazetteer of The United States and Canada,*

Betty McIntyre, Director, Dublin Public Library, Dublin, New Hampshire.

Jeanne M. Walsh, Reference Librarian, Brooks Memorial Library, Brattleboro, Vermont, Jennifer Ansart and other staff,

Richard E. Winslow III, historian emeritus, Portsmouth Public Library, Portsmouth, New Hampshire.

Source Abbreviations

References

ANB	*American National Biography*
DAB	*Dictionary of American Biography*
ODNB	*The Oxford Dictionary of National Biography*
WWW	*Who Was Who in America*

Henry James

HJL *Henry James Letters*, Leon Edel, ed. 4 vols. Cambridge, MA: Belknap Press of Harvard University Press, 1974-1984.

William James

CWJ *The Correspondence of William James.* Ignas K. Skrupskelis and Elizabeth M. Berkeley, eds. Wilma Bradbeer, assistant. 12 vols.Charlottesville: University Press of Virginia, 1992-2004. This is identified parenthetically by volume and page in text.

DWJ The Diary of William James. Houghton Library, Harvard University, Cambridge, Massachusetts. Microfilm.

ECR William James, *Essays, Comments, and Reviews.* Cambridge: Harvard University Press,1987.

HWJ *The Heart of William James.* Robert Richardson, ed. Cambridge: Harvard University Press, 2010.

WJR *William James Remembered.* Linda Simon, ed. Lincoln, Nebraska: University of Nebraska Press, 1996.

WJW 1   *William James: Writings:* 1878–1899. New York: The Library of America, 1992

WJW 2   *William James: Writings:* 1902–1910. New York: The Library of America, 1987.

Others

JMN   *The Journals and Miscellaneous Notebooks of Ralph Waldo Emerson.* William H. Gilman, R. H. Orth, et al, eds. 16 vols. Cambridge; Harvard University Press, 1960–1982.

LRF   *The Letters of Robert Frost, Volume* 1:1886–1920. Eds: Donald Sheehy, Mark Richardson, Robert Faggen. Cambridge, Massachusetts: The Belknap Press of Harvard University Press, 2014. (LRF)

LRK   *The Letters of Rudyard Kipling. Thomas Pinney, ed. 6 vols. Iowa City: University of Iowa Press,* 1990–2004. 1:1872–1889; 2:1890–1899; 3:1900–1910; 4:1911–1919; 5:1920–1930; 6:1931–1936.

NOTES

Prologue: Al Fresco Hours

1. Huber, *Wandering Apart: The Mountains of Henry James*, 2.

2. Isserman, *Continental Divide: A History of American Mountaineering*, 124.

3. Gifford, *Reconnecting with John Muir*, 143-145.

4. Huber, *A Wanderer*, 195 & 326n45. Letter, John Gerber to author, 20 May 2002. I am grateful for his checking the AMC membership register. Howard Palmer, "Early History of the American Alpine Club," *The American Alpine Journal*, 1944, 177.

5. Huber, *Elevating Ourselves*, 1 & 32.

6. Huber, *A Wanderer*, 201.

7. Wulf, *The Invention of Nature*, 80-89. Quotes:73, 83, 85, 87.

8. Simon, *Genuine Reality*, 117-118, Humboldt & WJ. Wulf, *The Invention of Nature*, 270-281; Edward Lurie, *Louis Agassiz*, 64-67, Humboldt & Agassiz. Habegger, *The Father*, 434. *Letters of William von Humboldt to a Female Friend* enchanted WJ. (1:79-81) Professor Irmscher, *Louis Agassiz*, shows just how supportive of Agassiz Humboldt was, 45-47, 83-84, and what a mountaineer Agassiz became while studying Swiss glaciers, 64-66.

9. See WJ on vacations in *North American Review* in *ECR*, 7; He advocated for vacations for all working people; even "vacation trusts." Also see WJ, "The Gospel of Relaxation," *HWJ*, 130-144.

10. "On a Certain Blindness in Human Beings," *HWJ*, 145-163. Pages given parenthetically in text. "The piece deserves a place among the defining documents of American democracy," Richardson wrote (145). See also Richardson, *WJ*, 381.

11. deeper desire of soul-life: Jefferies, *The Story of My Heart*, 16 & 140

(begins sentence with "Fullness," not "A". Both Jefferies and W.H. Hudson are in *ODNB*.

12. Thoreau, "Walking," *Excursions*, 189.

13. Thoreau, *Walden*, 111-112.

14. Thoreau, *The Maine Woods*, 70.

15. Moore, "The Truth of the Barnacles," 271, quote.

16. Habegger, Alfred, *The Father*. 44, "richest men" & 17, "leisured for life."

17. Habegger, *The Father*, 55-56; 66-82, loss of leg. Richardson, *WJ*, 29.

18. Habegger, *The Father*, 241, Hudson River.

19. Marsh, *Man and Nature*, 279-280. Elder, "Bushwhacking to the Source: The Most Influential Nature Book You've Never Read," *Northern Woodlands*, Spring 2016, 27-32.

20. Hiss, *In Motion*, 27.

Part One

In Sight of Monadnock

1. *Brattleboro Reformer*, 2 October 2013, 1&5, marriage cert. in bank, now in Rice-Aron Library, Marlboro College, Marlboro, Vermont. *The Commons* (Brattleboro, VT), 2 October 2013, B1&4.

2. Edel, *The Treacherous Years*, 4:48-50. *HJL* 3:364-365, HJ's assessment of Carrie at her brother's funeral.

3. *The Education of Henry Adams*, 319.

4. The Hunt-Hooker home was razed for retailers in spring 1929. Pliny Park, Windham Flowers, the Chamber of Commerce and Brown & Roberts Hardware now stand between High Street and the Baptist Church (1870). Jonathan Hunt was buried in Brattleboro's Prospect Hill Cemetery, as were William and Richard Morris Hunt. Baker, 9-11,14. For Colonel Hooker (1838-1902) see *Annals of Brattleboro* II: 812-815, and his file in Brattleboro Historical Society, which contains an obituary. I am indebted to John Carnahan and the late Joann Nichols for their assistance with the Hunts and Hookers of Brattleboro.

5. *The Vermont Phoenix* (weekly published in Brattleboro), 7 June 1895,

4, reports of laying of trolley road, begun 30 May, and of high temperatures. *LRK* 2:78, 174-175. The trolleys ran until 29 August 1923; their rails removed that fall (Shaw, *Trolley Days*)

6. I am indebted to my editor Susan Pollack and her husband Eric Schoonover for asking the meaning of Wantastiquet on 26 October 2013, and then supplying it from the internet, and to John and Mary Carnahan, who consulted Swift's *Vermont Place-Names*, 474, 477, 561.

7. *LRK* 2:187n3, 199n1, post office. Black Mountain: Wessels, *The Granite Landscape*, 12-18; *The Oak Log*, Nature Conservancy of Vermont, Spring/ Summer 2014, 4.

8. Henry Rutgers Marshall (1852-1927) is in *DAB*. The Kipling house name, however, reverses the "hk" of the novel's title. The novel was serialized in *The Century*, November 1891-July 1892. For Sunday tea, see Mary R. Cabot, "The Vermont Period: Rudyard Kipling at Naulakha," 169, 181. Cabot counted "Professor and Mrs. James" as one of the few "guests who came from a distance to Naulakha," 166.

9. Stewart, *Kipling's America*, 207-208. Andres & Johnson, *Buildings of Vermont*, 414.

10. Loss of Maplewood: Cabot, "The Vermont Period: Rudyard Kipling at Naulakha," 215; Mike Kipling, "Naulakha after Kipling," 27. *LRK* 2:175, "farming community."

11. *LRK* 2:163, to Henry James, 15 December 1894. Alice James was visiting the Salters in New Hampshire when WJ wrote her on 3 December 1894 (7:619). I presume, therefore, the Kiplings visited after that date.

12. *LRK* 2: 179, RK says "nearly six weeks" in WA. 2:187n3, with Cleveland 5 April; 2:188n1, 6-7 April in NY on their return. Morris, *Theodore Roosevelt*, 476-477, 479, with TR 7 March. Cabot, "The Vermont Period: Rudyard Kipling at Naulakha," 178, Washington.

13. *LRK* 2:180, liverwort and maple sugar.

14. "Spring Running" is the last story of *The Second Jungle Book*, which the *Century* published on 10 November 1895, architect Henry Rutgers Marshall informed, 8:95-96. *The Jungle Book* had appeared to acclaim on 24 May 1894. Its violence upset Henry James; see Ricketts, 205, and Edel, *The Middle Years*, 380. In August 1893, Kipling began writing *The Jungle Book*, at the Bliss Cottage, which they rented until Naulakha was ready for them in August 1893 (see note 19 below).

Both WJ & HJ read Kipling and expressed their reactions in letters to each other. See Edel 4:50-53; Daniel Mark Fogel, 2: xxxii-xxxiii; WJ read "The Light that Failed," in *Lippincott's Monthly Magazine*, January 1891; another version appeared in book form of March 1891, 7:140-141n5 (2:176n2 incorrectly dates book at 1890). WJ to HJ, 15 February 1891, 2:174-175. In introduction to Kipling's collection of stories, *Mine Own People* (March 1891) HJ praised Kipling's resources—freshness, knowledge, invention, "lyric string and the patriotic chord"; see Ricketts, 182-183.

15. Pinney, *The Cambridge Edition of the Poems of Rudyard Kipling*, 1:367-370.

16. Letter, John Walker to J. Parker Huber, 26 May 2010.

17. *LRK* 2:260n2. Kipling, *Something of Myself*, 70, guardian mountain.

18. Taliaferro, *All the Great Prizes: The Life of John Hay*, 295. Thorson, *Beyond Walden*, 28, Lake Sunapee, "ice-gashed bedrock basin."

19. *LRK* 2:122-123, dispute; 55n1 & 106n2 The Kiplings stayed in Bliss Cottage for a year, from 10 August 1892 to 12 August 1893, when they moved up the road a half-mile to Naulakha. Relocated and part of World Learning campus, Bliss Cottage still stands.

as pretty as eye could wish

1. I am grateful to Peter Davis for our conversation of 16 August 2011 about the Lawrence farm. *History of Jaffrey* (Town of Jaffrey, 1934), I: 378, 486. Dori Jones, "Jaffrey's Monadnock Inn," *Leisure* (Keene, NH), 10-16 July 1980.

2. Watermans, *Forest and Crag*, 233-234, Monadnock trails. The profusion of paths from the Half Way House came later, 1890 to 1910. Mountain House became the Half Way House in 1916, according to Chamberlain, *Annals*, 37. Brandon, *Monadnock*, 111-113, Pumpelly trail & photo of him with long beard. Baldwin, *Monadnock Guide*, 95. For Pumpelly, see *DAB*, *ANB* & Champlin's biography. Champlin 131, description of him. Morgan, *Monadnock Summer*, 45, 51(illustrated), 74-75 (illustrated), his wooden Dublin home burned in 1919. An Italian villa of stucco walls and tile roof, Pompelia, replaced it until 1979, when vandals torched it. A one-half-mile path led south from the Pumpelly home to the Pumpelly trail.

3. Champlin, 153-158, Green Mountain survey.

4. 1870 Census, Pumpelly address thanks to Alyssa Pacy, archivist,

Cambridge Public Library, and Harvard University Archives, General catalogue and "A Literary Map of Cambridge," (n.d.) by Wendy H. Chang, et al. Howe, *Later Years of the Saturday Club*, 188-192, profile. *Historical Register of Harvard University, 1636-1936.* (Cambridge: Harvard University, 1937) 369.

5. Pumpelly Glacier, Joan Hamilton, "Parks as Arks," *Sierra*, September-October 2009, 48-54. Champlin, 112-113: "he never published anything about this discovery nor, apparently, did he campaign for the creation of the park, although he obviously appreciated its beauty." Pumpelly, *Reminiscences*, 638-646. Accompanying him were horticulturist Charles S. Sargent and botanist William M. Canby, both close friends of John Muir, who would have been along had he not to provide for his new family by fruit farming in Martinez these years. The glacial evidence Pumpelly had found on Mount Baglia Orba, Corsica, in 1856-1857 he did publish, but this was his first and only time, Champlin says, 15.

6. Dorr, *The Story of Acadia National Park*, 13-15.

7. The best source on Alexander James is R.W.B. Lewis, *The Jameses*, 625-631. Lewis spells Thayer's first name with one "t" and his second with an "e" (Hend . . .) instead of an "a." A son of Aleck and Frederika James, Alexander Robertson James Jr ("Sandy," 1918-1995), became an architect (Yale, 1948) and designed several homes in Dublin. See Lewis, 631-632, Morgan, *Monadnock Summer*, 116-117.

At the portals of that Adirondack wilderness

1. Henry Van Hoevenberg (1849-1918): 8:46, 568; Donaldson, *History of the Adirondacks*, 23-28; Duquette, 6; Hicks, 75-81.

Colorado has now become a part of my Self

1. See, Huber, *A Wanderer*, 266n7; 34-36, for David and Mabel Loomis Todd at 1893 Colorado Summer School. Scott gives background on Mrs. Elizabeth Cass Goddard (1840-1918, nee Ledyard). She and her son, Henry Ledyard Goddard, moved from Providence, Rhode Island, to Colorado Springs in 1887. Her husband died on 16 May 1889; her son, on 30 August 1892. First Congregational Church Welcome Booklet (the one I saw in August 2010 was undated); www.fcucc.org. Thoreau, *Reform Papers*, 4.

2. Henry Rutgers Marshall (1852-1927) is in *DAB*. Marshall's philosophical-psychological work became his focus after his wife's death in 1888. (7:225-226) James's review of his *Aesthetic Principles* appeared in the *Nation*, 12 September 1895, 192-193, and is in *ECR*, 518-519. He had read Marshall's *Pain, Pleasure, and Aesthetics* (1894) and reviewed it for the *Nation*, 17 July 1894, 49-51; also in *ECR*, 489-493. (7:525-526; 519-520n3). First Congregational Church Welcome Booklet (above).

3. Tweit, "A Beautiful Resurrection," 42-48, and *Walking Nature Home*, 158-161. In 2017 Susan Tweit moved to Cody, Wyoming.

4. Benson, *Colorado Place Names*, Marshall Pass, 133, was named for Lt. William L. Marshall of Wheeler Survey in 1873, not architect Henry Rutgers Marshall; for Mount Harvard, 148.

5. Colorado: Stewart, *Kipling's America*, 140, Letter 15, 4 March 1890, "mad ride." Stewart also says (xxv) that both Ruddy and Caroline had been in the American West (Colorado) that "provided half the setting for *The Naulahka*."; Likely Colorado was a topic of conversation when the Jameses and Kiplings convened at Naulakha.

infinite good: a fine ten days in Keene Valley

1. *Adirondack Trails: High Peaks Region* (Lake George, New York: Adirondack Mountain Club, 2004), 45, "triple-crested mountain."

2. There is some question about when WJ made his first trip to Keene Valley. According to Richard Plunz, *Two Adirondack Hamlets*, 202, it was 1874 when two Putnam brothers, James Jackson and Charles Pickering, Henry Pickering Bowditch & WJ arrived. Earlier in the same book, 111, Elizabeth Coutrier Andrews, says they arrived in 1873. Prochnik, *Putnam Camp*, 30, says in "1870s" (not giving the exact date), the Putnams, Henry Bowditch, and WJ made "walking trips through the New York State mountains . . . happened at last upon Keene Valley." Prochnik's source is his grandmother, Putnam's eldest daughter, Elizabeth—her 1941 address to Keene Valley Historical Society.

   Simon, *Genuine Reality*, 156, places the two Bowditch brothers (Henry Pickering and Charles Pickering) with James Jackson Putnam & WJ at Putnam Camp in 1875. Simon, *WJR*, 7, has two Putnam brothers, with Bowditch & WJ.

   The Adirondack Reader (3rd ed. 2009), 399 & 415, says Putnam Camp was purchased from Smith Beede in 1877.

3. 1876: Simon, *Genuine Reality*, 158.

4. Honeymoon: Gunter, *Alice in Jamesland*, 56-58; Richardson,190; 5:18-20; 5:17, Putnam cottage rental; 5:521, Grand Union Hotel; 8:378, Lake George sail; WJ's letter of 12 September from Keene Valley has been lost, 1:307.

5. Gunter, *Alice in Jamesland*, 152-153. Josephine Clara Goldmark, "An Adirondack Friendship, *WJR*, 172-173.

PART TWO
The Green Mountains of Vermont

1. Habegger, *The Father*, 452.

2. Joseph Battell, *The Yankee Boy from Home* (New York: James Miller, 1864). Pages appear parenthetically in text.

3. Huber, *Wandering Apart*, 2.

4. I am still in search of Bertha Mountain, and would appreciate hearing from anyone who knows its location. Allaire Diamond to J. Parker Huber, 18 July 2016. I am indebted to Allaire Diamond, conservation ecologist with the Vermont Land Trust, for her dedicated pursuit of its whereabouts.

5. Albers, "The Greening of the Green Mountain State," *The Vermont Difference*,84.

6. Joseph Battell (1839-1915), *WWW, The Vermont Encyclopedia*; Albers, "The Greening of the Green Mountain State," *The Vermont Difference*, 83-101. For Breadloaf Inn, see Andres and Johnson, *Buildings of Vermont*, 128. In the decade following WJ's stays, architect Clinton G. Smith began remodeling the inn, adding a barn and "two large annexes (1885) with porches and galleries."Andres & Johnson also tell us of Battell Block and Bridge in Middlebury (1892-1898),122. Bain & Duffy, *Whose Woods These Are*, 4-13, encapsulates well Battell's life. Authors believe that Battell read *Man and Nature* by George Perkins Marsh of Woodstock, Vermont, published in May 1864—the same year as Battell's *Yankee Boy from Home* (8-9)—which within a decade became "an international classic," Marsh's biographer David Lowenthall states (302).Robert McCullough, Clare Ginger, and Michelle Baumflek, "Unspoiled Vermont," 135-137, in Foster, *Twentieth-Century New England Land Conservation*, view Battell as leader of movement to protect state's forests. As state legislator, they say, Battell proposed a forestry

commission, which was created in 1882. According to them, Battell acquired the inn in 1865 and opened it five years later. I use 1866 date for both purchase and opening that Bain & Duffy give.

7. Robert McCullough, Clare Ginger, and Michelle Baumflek, "Unspoiled Vermont," 135-137, in Foster, *Twentieth-Century New England Land Conservation*, 162-163, and *Long Trail Guide* (2011), 8, 129.

8. A book on "The Mountains of RF" would be welcome. A few excursions will suffice here. In summer 1895 RF rented a cabin on Ossipee Mountains off the northeast end of Lake Winnipesaukee, NH. In 1909 Frost had camped with his family at Lake Willoughby in northeastern Vermont, connecting with ferns and mounts Pisgah (2,751 feet) on the lake's east side and Hor (2,848 feet) on the other. In spring 1914 on, in Ledbury, Gloucestershire, where the Frosts rented a cottage called Little Iddens, RF climbed May Hill four miles distant and almost one thousand feet high, first with British poet Edward Thomas, with whom a close friendship matured. Living in Franconia, New Hampshire (June 1915 to January 1917; summers: 1917-1918) RF had splendid views of the White Mountains, especially Lafayette (5,260 feet), with whom he and Charles Lowell Young spent a day atop. Parini, 4, 12-13; Thompson, *Early Years*, Hor & Pisgah, 350-354. May Hill with Thomas, 447-448, 455, "repeated climbs." *LRF*,1:597-599, Lafayette.

9. WJ gave Gifford Lectures in May-June 1901; and the second series, the following spring.

10. Thompson, *Early Years*, 238, states incorrectly that WJ was on leave due to illness, 1898-1899. Richardson, 380 & 382, says WJ was teaching full-time academic year, 1898-1899, despite cardiac concerns. Simon, *Genuine Reality*, 290, says he ended college year in spring 1899, "feeling hopeful and energetic," planned sabbatical in Europe to write Giffords to be delivered in January 1900.(290) Parini, 61-66, says the influence of WJ on RF was "profound." He repeats Thompson on James's absence from teaching, 1898-1899. *LRF* 1:42-43n42; quote, 764; this volume contains no letters written during RF's Harvard years, 1897-1899. Munsterberg's *Psychology and Life* (189?) did not impress James (8:633).

11. Long Trail: Thompson, *The Years of Triumph*, 188-201 & [Lesley Frost], "Long Trail, 225." Though unsigned, Thompson, 199, says Lesley Frost wrote this account, as does the Frost House Museum,

South Shaftsbury. Lesley Frost says from Middlebury Gap they went down to the Bread Loaf Inn to reprovision; less Frost, I presume, who wanted to avoid contact with the Bread Loaf School of English in session at the inn. For Frost and Charles Lowell Young in Peru in 1918, see *LRF* 1:623. Parini, *RF*, 214, relates that on Pico Peak Frost's foot problem required him to leave the Long Trail. Pico Peak, however—about half way between Killington Peak to the south and Shelburne Pass (Route 4) to the north—was part of the trail that Frost did not tramp. Parini also writes that Frost reached Mt. Mansfield, which is fifty-one miles north of where Frost left the Long Trail at Lincoln Gap to walk the roads north. No one of the original party of six reaches the "Canadian border" for the trail stopped at Smuggler's Notch (Route 108)—their intended destination, which they reached without Frost.

12. Noble Farm: Parini, *RF*, 327. Bill McKibben and Sue Halpern built their home on land once owned by RF in Ripton, close to Frost's writing cabin. McKibben, *Wandering Home*, 12.

These Alps are Absolutely Medicinal: Switzerland

1. Huber, *Wandering Apart*, 17. HJ on Faulhorn in 1872.

2. WJ does not say which Scheideck, Kleine or Grosse; judging by the direction he is going it is Grosse. I am indebted to Edwin Bruijn of Brattleboro, Vermont, who has climbed in this region of the Bernese Alps.

3. Huber, *Wandering Apart*, 9, HJ on Scheideck in 1869.

4. Huber, *A Wanderer All My Days*, 46, Muir with Royce in Cambridge; 55-56, Muir, Gornergrat.

The White Mountains of New Hampshire and the Adirondacks

1. Erastus Brigham Bigelow is in *DAB*. For Stonehurst, see Tolles, *Summer Cottages*, 15-19.

2. Hirshler, *A Studio of Her Own*, 31, 33, 34 (Helen Merriman's portrait of Whitman), 39, 160n3 (students of William Morris Hunt). Later, c. 1906, Helen painted a portrait of Sarah Wyman Whitman, which is in the Schlesinger Library in Cambridge, MA. This is only painting of hers at Harvard, Marylène Altieri, Curator of Books and Printed Materials at the Schlesinger Library, informed (letter, 11 August 2010). In August 1898 (8:412, 421), Helen also executed

portraits of WJ's wife, Alice James (1849-1922) and/or their daughter Peggy (Margaret Mary James Porter,1887-1950), which I have not located.There is no published history of the Worcester Art Museum, librarian Debbie Aframe informed on 8 April 2015; nor does the museum contain any works by Helen Merriman. See James Welu, "Helen Bigelow Merriman and the Worcester Art Museum," undated.

3. I am indebted to Bob Spoerl, Land Agent, NH Forest and Lands, Concord, NH, for information and map of Merriman State Forest in August 2010. His records show that Mildred H. & Alfonso T. Kimball gave an additional section of the forest in August 1919. The map of April 2002 indicates the size is 505 acres.

4. Adolf Meyer, *DAB*; Roger Merriman (1876-1945), *WWW*.

5. I draw from Susan Gunter's fine description of this place, wishing I could see it for myself; *Alice in Jamesland*, 177, 178. When James visited the Merrimans at Stonehurst, 27-30 September 1901, though they were outdoors, no climbing was noted. (9:548,637)

6. Huber, *A Wanderer All My Days*, 88.

7. Gunter, 157; Nickerson, *Chocorua Peak House*, passim, 24. On 26 September 1915, "a gale of unusual velocity" blew away the cable-anchored Peak House. Jim Liberty Cabin is now located there. *AMC White Mountain Guide*, 26th edition, 326, says 1891 Peak House was two-story.

8. Lefcowitz, 321-322. *ODNB* for Bryce (1838-1922) and his father (1806-1877) and grandfather (1767-1857), a Scottish Presbyterian minister.

9. Lefcowitz, 322. McAleer, 552-555. Stillman's portrait of Emerson et al, which Judge Rockwood Hoar bought and gave to the Concord Free Public Library, is still there.

10. Lefcowitz, 323-324.

11. *JMN* 16:194, 6 September 1870 itinerary. Lefcowitz, 325-326.

The Biggest Tramp

1. First Fort William Henry Hotel was completely destroyed by fire on 24 June 1909: Tolles, *Resort Hotels of the Adirondacks*, 30-38. First Hotel Champlain consumed by fire on 25 May 1910: Tolles, ibid., 64-72, quote, 68. Richard B. Frost, *Hotel Champlain to Clinton Community College*, 27-28; 13 & 41, *Harper's Weekly* cover, 16 August

1890.

2. Thomas Davidson (1840-1900) is in *ANB* & *DAB*. See WJ, "Thomas Davidson: Individualist," *ECR*, 86-97. Davidson bought 200 acres in 1889 and founded Glenmore Summer School in 1890. Plunz, *Two Adirondack Hamlets*, 216-217. James stayed at Glenmore for first time in June 1895; Davidson as innkeeper and the beauty of the place impressed him. (8:46-47) Davidson first introduced WJ to Alice Gibbens in 1876, according to Richardson, *WJ*, 168.

The Sierra Nevada of California

1. For capsule of WJ itinerary west, 3:39-40n1.

2. Thoreau, *The Maine Woods*. Pages given parenthetically.

3. Seattle Hills: *Lonely Planet*.

4. Archie Hobson, *The Cambridge Gazetteer of the United States and Canada* (New York: Cambridge University Press,1995) indicated that San Francisco has over forty hills, but these seven are the most prominent. Solnit, *Wanderlust*,171-175, 194-195, began walking San Francisco streets as a teenager. "To me, the magic of the street is the mingling of the errand and the epiphany," 178. She considers various landscapes where people walk: streets, gardens, mountains. Muir and Thoreau are here, but not WJ.

5. Albert Kellogg is in *DAB* & *ANB*. Gunter, *Alice in Jamesland*, 6-7.

6. At this time Charles Montague Bakewell (1867-1957) was an instructor in philosophy at University of California, Berkeley; he had been the same at Harvard 1896-1897, from where he had graduated: BA in 1892, PhD in 1894. *WWW*. Sargent, *Wawona*, 17, Albert Henry Washburn, born in Randolph, Vermont, 17 November 1836. His father, Seth Washburn (1788-1841) was born in Putney, Vermont, to where family returned upon his death.

7. Fox, *John Muir*, 3-7, Muir-Emerson meeting. Muir, *The Mountains of California*, 108-115.

8. Sargent, *Wawona*, 10, shows the six upper cascades of Chilnualna Falls in an 1891 photograph.

9. Sargent, *Wawona*, 16, 25, South Fork Road replaced 24-mile horse trail.

10. Geologist Clarence King named the peak for John Conness, the

US senator who secured Yosemite Valley and Mariposa Grove of Big Trees for his state of California to be "held for public use, resort, and recreation . . . inalienable for all time," which President Lincoln approved on 30 June 1864. Five years later, in 1869—Muir's first Sierra summer—Conness left the Senate on 3 March, and two weeks later, 16 March, married Mary Russell Davis, in her native town, Greenfield, Massachusetts: she twenty-two, he forty-seven; her first marriage, his second. As of 8 July 1870, they lived in New York City. By the next year, they had moved to River Street in Lower Mills in Mattapan, which is now part of Boston. He lived here to his death in 1909. On 4 April 1895, he visited Muir at his Martinez, California, home. *Who Was Who* (1821-1909). Wilkins, *Clarence King*, 89, Mt. Conness. Browning, *Place Names of the Sierra Nevada*, 44-45, says Whitney Survey named peak in 1863. For Yosemite Grant see Reid, *Treasury of the Sierra Nevada*, 317-318; and 314-316 for Israel Ward Raymond's letter to Conness of 20 February 1864, which along with a selection of Carleton E. Watkins photographs, urged the preservation of these two places. Conness is not in *CWJ*.

11. Shields, Allan, "William James Visits Yosemite in 1898," *Yosemite Association*, Summer 2001, 6-9.

12. Mark Twain Letter, 9 October 1905, in *Where the Mountain Stands Alone*, 205. Simon, *Genuine Reality*, 64, 77, 79-80; 85-87, WJ's career decision. Richardson, *WJ*, 38-40, 43, sees value of WJ's art study to cultivate his capacity to pay attention. Science, however, called louder and fall 1861 found WJ at Lawrence Scientific School, which had "no requirements for admission," Richardson says.

13. Sargent, *Wawona*, 39, 41. *Consuming Views: Art & Tourism in the White Mountains, 1850-1900*, Concord, NH: New Hampshire Historical Society, 2006, 46-47, Thomas Hill, *Crawford Notch* (1872) and 72-73, *Mount Lafayette in Winter* (1870, also painted Mount Chocorua) and Edward Hill, *Franconia Notch, White Mts.—Echo Lake and Profile House* (1887).

14. Kimes, 64-65, "sermons in stones" and Emerson-Muir meeting. Huber, *A Wanderer*, 191 & 323n29 for Muir & WJ in *Atlantic*; and WJ in Sierra. WJ did not appear in any of these 1899-1900 *Atlantic* issues with Muir. Wessels, *Granite Landscape*, 157-170; quote,159. There is no correspondence between Muir and WJ; no mention of Muir in *CWJ* & none of James in Muir's letters that I have read. Fox, *John*

Muir, 88.

15. Gunter, *Alice in Jamesland,* 225, visit to Mountain View; 228, "old country road"; Her source is Gay Wilson Allen, *William James,* 455, who used Alice's diary of 26 April 1906, which has disappeared, according to Gunter, 337n61. Philip L. Fradkin, *The Great Earthquake,* 145-147, for Alice's letter of 18 April 1906.

Mount Marcy Redux, 1899

1. Distinctive step: *WJR,* 15.

2. . Joe: *Adirondack Trails: High Peaks Region* (Lake George, New York: Adirondack Mountain Club, 2004), 141.

PART THREE
1903 — *Asheville, North Carolina*

1. Martin Filler, "America's Green Giant," *New York Review,* 5 November 2015, 12, 14, 16 (quote).

2. William James, "A Charming North Carolina Resort," *ECR,* 133-135. See Huber, *A Wanderer All My Days,* 195-196.

1904 — *Henry James at Chocorua*

1. Henry James, *The American Scene* in *Collected Travel Writings: Great Britain and America* (New York: Library of America, 1993). Pages given parenthetically in text (*AS*). Huber, *Wandering Apart: The Mountains of Henry James,* 23-24.

1905 – *Greece and Hancock, New Hampshire*

1. Harlow, *Perry,* 182 (quote)-185, farm purchase. *DAB* entry of Thomas Sergeant Perry is by poet Edwin Arlington Robinson, whose portrait Lilla Perry painted in 1916, see Martindale, *Lilla Cabot Perry,* 133.

2. Clark, *Time Travel,* 16-17 Tuttle-Perry-Moffat House photos.

3. Harlow, *Perry,* 203 & 204, HJ visit & naming Flagstones happened after WJ's death in August 1910. Martindale, *Lilla Cabot Perry,* 86, agrees. 1911 HJ letters in Harlow, 330-333, reveal HJ's tight schedule before leaving for England on 30 July prohibited his accepting Perry's invitation to Hancock. My Flagstones visits with the Moffats occurred on 2 September 2010 and 4 August 2011. The

latter date's walk to Juggernaut Pond is related in Huber, *Living by Loving*, 233-234.

4. Martindale, *Lilla Cabot Perry*, 53. *The Trio*.

5. Joseph Clark Grew (1880-1965) and Jay Pierrepont Moffat (1896-1943)are in *WWW*.

6. Harris Center: James C. Collins and Richard Ober, "New Hampshire: Common Ground," in *Foster, Twentieth-Century New England Land Conservation*, 117-118. Hancock History Committee, *The Second Hundred Years of Hancock, New Hampshire* (Canaan, New Hampshire: Phoenix Publishing 1979), 17-18, 108-109.

7. Thomas Sergeant Perry, *John Fiske* (Boston: Small, Maynard, 1906). Harlow, *Thomas Sergeant Perry*, 183-185.

8. Martindale, *Lilla Cabot Perry*, 100, *Mist on the Mountain*.

1908 — *Lake District*

1. William Wordsworth, *Guide to the Lakes*. ed. Ernest de Sélincourt. (London & New York: Oxford University Press, 1977). Pages given parenthetically. This is reprint of 1835 edition; see Introduction, iii-vi.

2. *WJR*, 217, "James had read all of Wordsworth." *WJ Writings: 1878-1899*, 501, 849, 983, 1087, "an eternal order."

3. For Ruskin (1819-1900) see *ODNB*. Richardson, *WJ*, 448, says that WJ also read Ruskin's letters to Charles Eliot Norton, as they appeared in the *Atlantic Monthly* in 1904, and his memoir, *Praeterita*, vol. 35 of *The Works of John Ruskin*, ed. E. T.Cook and A. Wedderburn (London: George Allen, 1908). Alice's father gave her a copy of Ruskin's *Modern Painters*, Gunter, *Jamesland*, 14.This was published in five volumes, 1843-1860.

4. Lear, *Beatrix Potter*, quote, 216, 218-220, 222-223, Lear relates the features in *Jemima Puddle-Duck*. *Beatrix Potter's Letters*, 159-162, for Potter's whereabouts in 1908.

5. Wilson's 1906 visit: A. Wilson, *A President's Love Affair with the Lake District*, 19-25; quotes, Gowbarrow Park, 21, and "the region we most love," 19.

6. Wilson's 1896 visit: Berg, *Wilson*, 124-125, and A. Wilson, *A President's Love Affair with the Lake District*, 6-7.

7. Wilson's 1908 visit: A. Wilson, *A President's Love Affair with the*

Lake District, 26-38. Quotes from *Papers of Woodrow Wilson* (*PWW*) given parenthetically in text.

8. William Mackintire Salter is in *DAB* & *ANB*. On 2 December 1885 William Salter wed Mary Sherwin Gibbens, Alice James's middle sister. Hill Top on Old Salter Hill Road, now Jenks Road, was their summer home.

1909 — Freud and Jung in Keene Valley

1. Rosenzweig, *Freud, Jung,* gives overview of topics of delivered and published versions,125-134, and the lectures themselves, 397-438.

2. See Freud's letter of 16 September in Hale, *James Jackson Putnam and Psychoanalysis,* 23-24. Prochnik, *Putnam Camp,*18 & 21, says Putnam, arriving just hours before his guests on 15 September, met their conveyance at 2:30 P.M and invited them to hike the mountain that afternoon. Rosenzweig, *Freud, Jung,*256, has Putnam's arrival on the 16 September, which is a rainy rest day, according to Freud's letter.

3. Freud's letter of 16 September says that they were leaving the day after tomorrow, and would be in New York that evening.

4. Prochnik, *Putnam Camp,* 366-367, 376. The nine-year Freud-Putnam relationship, begun at Putnam Camp, focused on the future of psychoanalysis in America. In Freud's preface to Putnam's *Addresses* (1921), Freud described Putnam as "the first American to interest himself in psycho-analysis," who soon became "its most decided supporter and its most influential representative in America."

Bibliography

The Education of Henry Adams. 1918: Boston & New York: A Mariner Book/ Houghton Miffllin, 2000.

Albers, Jan. *Hands on the Land: A History of the Vermont Landscape.* Cambridge, MA: MIT Press, 2000.

Allen, Gay Wilson. *William James: A Biography.* New York: Viking Press, 1967.

Andres, Glenn M. and Curtis B. Johnson. *Buildings of Vermont.* Charlottesville: University of Virginia Press, 2014.

Bain, David Howard, and Mary Smyth Duffy. *Whose Woods These Are: A History of the Bread Loaf Writers' Conference, 1926-1992.* Hopewell, New Jersey: Ecco Press, 1993.

Baker, Paul R. *Richard Morris Hunt.* Cambridge, MA: MIT Press, 1980.

Baldwin, Henry I. *Monadnock Guide.* Concord, New Hampshire: Society for the Protection of New Hampshire Forests, 1980.

Benson, Maxine. 1001 *Colorado Place Names.* Lawrence: University Press of Kansas, 1994.

Berg, A. Scott. *Wilson.* New York: G.P. Putnam's Sons, 2013.

Brandon, Craig. *Monadnock: More than a Mountain.* Keene, New Hampshire: Surry Cottage Books, 2007.

Browning, Peter. *Place Names of the Sierra Nevada.* Berkeley, California: Wilderness Press, 1986.

Cabot, Mary R. *Annals of Brattleboro, 1681-1895.* 2 vols. Brattleboro, Vermont: E.L. Hildreth, 1922.

Cabot, Mary R. "The Vermont Period: Rudyard Kipling at Naulakha," *English Literature in Transition, 1880-1920,* v.29, #2, 1986, 161-218.

Cenkl, Pavel. *The Vast Book of Nature: Writing the Landscape of New*

Hampshire's White Mountains, 1784-1911. Iowa City: University of Iowa Press, 2006.

Chamberlain, Allen. *The Annals of the Grand Monadnock.* 1936; Concord: Society for the Protection of New Hampshire Forests, 1975.

Champlin, Peggy [Margaret D.]. *Raphael Pumpelly: Gentleman Geologist of the Gilded Age.* Tuscaloosa, Alabama: The University of Alabama Press, 1994.

Clark, Francelia, with Pam Godin. *Time Travel with Horses.* Hollis, NH: Puritan Press, 2007.

Donaldson, Alfred L. *A History of the Adirondacks.* New York: The Century Co., 1921.

Dorr, George B. *The Story of Acadia National Park.* Bar Harbor, Maine: Acadia Press, 1997; 3rd edition).

Duquette, John J. "Henry Van Hoevenbergh's life in region," *Adirondack Daily Enterprise,* Saranac Lake, New York, 5 December 1986. Photographs of lodge and Van Hoevenberg, whose name originally ended with h.

Edel, Leon. *Henry James: The Untried Years,* 1843-1870. *The Conquest of London,* 1870-1881. *The Middle Years,* 1882-1895. *The Treacherous Years,* 1895-1901. *The Master,* 1901-1916. 5 vols. Philadelphia and New York: J. B.Lippincott, 1953-1972.

Elder, John. "Bushwhacking to the Source: The Most Influential Nature Book You've Never Read," *Northern Woodlands,* Spring 2016.

Foster, Charles H. W., ed. *Twentieth-Century New England Land Conservation.* Petersham, Massachusetts: Harvard Forest, 2009.

Fox, Stephen. *John Muir and His Legacy: The American Conservation Movement.* Boston: Little, Brown, 1981.

Fradkin, Philip L. *The Great Earthquake and Firestorms of* 1906. Berkeley & Los Angeles: University of California Press, 2005.

[Lesley Frost] "Long Trail, 225 Miles, Yields to Youth and Vigor," *Bennington Evening Banner,* 12 September 1922, 1.

Frost, Richard B., *Hotel Champlain to Clinton Community College: A Chronicle of Bluff Point.* Virginia Beach, Virginia: Donning Company, 2011.

Robert Frost: Collected Poems, Prose, & Plays. New York: The Library of

America, 1995.

Gifford, Terry. *Reconnecting with John Muir: Essays in Post-Pastoral Practice*. Athens, Georgia: University of Georgia Press, 2006

Guyon, Anne Lawrence, "The House (in Vermont) Where Mowgli Grew Up," NYT, 19 March 2010, C33-34. Color Photographs of Naulakha interior/exterior. Naulakha, now owned by Landmark Trust USA, can be rented for three days to three weeks. This article gives information on renting and visiting Brattleboro.

Habegger, Alfred. *The Father: A Life of Henry James, Sr.* 1994; Amherst, MA: University of Massachusetts Press, 2001.

Hale, Jr, Nathan G. *James Jackson Putnam and Psychoanalysis*. Cambridge, MA: Harvard University Press, 1971.

Harlow, Virginia. *Thomas Sergeant Perry: A Biography*. Durham, NC: Duke University Press, 1950.

Hicks, Harry Wade. "Henry Van Hoevenberg," *The Adirondack Mountain Club Annual*, January 1940, 75-81.

Hirshler, Erica E. *A Studio of Her Own: Women Artists in Boston, 1870-1940*. Boston: MFA Publications, 2001.

Hiss, Tony. *In Motion: The Experience of Travel*. New York: Alfred A. Knopf, 2010.

Howe, M.A. DeWolf, ed. *Later Years of the Saturday Club, 1870-1920*. Freeport, NY: Books for Libraries Press, 1968.

Huber, J. Parker, ed. *Elevating Ourselves: Henry David Thoreau on Mountains*. Boston: Houghton Mifflin, 1999.

Huber, J. Parker. *Living by Loving: Journal of a Solitude at Seventy*. Brattleboro, Vermont: privately printed, 2012.

Huber, J. Parker. *A Wanderer All My Days: John Muir in New England*. Sheffield, Vermont: Green Frigate Books, 2006.

Huber, J. Parker. *Wandering Apart: The Mountains of Henry James*. Brattleboro, Vermont: privately printed, 2014. Available at Mortimer Rare Book Room of Neilson Library, Smith College, Northampton, Massachusetts, and other libraries.

Hyman, Tom. *"Village on a Hill. A History of Dublin, New Hampshire, 1752-2000*. Peterborough, New Hampshire: Peter E. Randall, 2002.

Irmscher, Christoph. *Louis Agassiz: Creator of American Science*. Boston/New York: Houghton Mifflin Harcourt, 2013.

Isserman, Maurice. *Continental Divide: A History of American Mountaineering.* New York: W.W. Norton, 2016.

Jefferies, Richard. *The Story of My Heart as Rediscovered by Brooke Williams and Terry Tempest Williams.* Salt Lake City, Utah: Torrey House Press, 2014.

Kilbourne, Frederick W. "Chocorua: The Complete Mountain." *Appalachia,* December 1942, 155-166. Testimonies of Chocorua's uniqueness. Chocorua's preeminent poet is John Greenleaf Whittier (1807-1892), author says; Whittier did not climb mountains. Whittier and Alice James were friends from 1874 until his death; see Gunter for their relationship, 29,30, 49, 55-56, 189.

Kimes, William F. and Maymie B. Kimes. *John Muir: A Reading Bibliography.* 1978; Fresno, California: Panorama West, 1986.

Kipling, Mike, "Naulakha After Kipling," *Kipling Journal,* September 2013, 20-36.

Kipling, Rudyard. *Something of Myself for My Friends Known and Unknown.* Garden City, New York: Doubleday, Doran, 1937.

Kipling, Rudyard, with Wolcott Balestier. *The Naulahka: A Story of West and East.* New York & London: Macmillan, 1892.

Lurie, Edward. *Louis Agassiz: A Life in Science.* 1960; Baltimore, MD: The Johns Hopkins University Press, 1988.

Lear, Linda. *Beatrix Potter: A Life in Nature.* New York: St. Martin's Press, 2007.

Lefcowitz, Allan B. and Barbara F., "James Bryce's First Visit to America: The New England Sections of His 1870 Journal and Related Correspondence," *New England Quarterly,* June 1977, 314-331. An abridgment appeared in *Appalachia,* June 1979, 97-100.

Lewis, R.W.B. *The Jameses: A Family Narrative.* New York: Farrar, Straus and Giroux, 1991.

Marsh, George Perkins. *Man and Nature.* David Lowenthal, ed. Cambridge, MA: The Belknap Press of Harvard University Press, 1974.

Martindale, Meredith, with Pamela Moffat. *Lilla Cabot Perry: An American Impressionist.* Washington, DC: The National Museum of Women in the Arts, 1990.

McAleer, John. *Ralph Waldo Emerson: Days of Encounter.* Boston: Little, Brown, 1984.

McKibben, Bill. *Wandering Home: A Long Walk Across America's Most Hopeful Landscape: Vermont's Champlain Valley and New York's Adirondacks.* New York: Crown Journeys, 2005.

Moore, Kathleen Dean. "The Truth of the Barnacles: Rachel Carson and the Moral Significance of Wonder," *Environmental Ethics*, Fall 2005, 265-77.

Morgan, William. *Monadnock Summer: The Architectural Legacy of Dublin, New Hampshire.* Jaffrey NH: David R. Godine, 2011.

Morris, Edmund. *The Rise of Theodore Roosevelt.* New York: Coward, McCann & Geoghegan, 1979.

Muir, John. *The Mountains of California.* Edward Hoagland, intro. 1894; New York: Penguin, 1985.

Murray, Stuart. *Rudyard Kipling in Vermont: Birthplace of The Jungle Books.* Bennington, VT: Images from the Past, 1997.

Nickerson, Marion L. and John A. Downs. *Chocorua Peak House.* Center Conway, NH: Walker's Pond Press, 1977). Copy in Special Collections, Mason Library, Keene State College, Keene, NH.

Pinney, Thomas, ed. *The Cambridge Edition of the Poems of Rudyard Kipling.* 3vols. New York: Cambridge University Press, 2013.

Pinney, Thomas, ed. *Rudyard Kipling: Something of Myself and Other Autobiographical Writings.* Cambridge: Cambridge University Press, 1990.

Plunz, Richard, ed. *Two Adirondack Hamlets in History: Keene and Keene Valley.* Fleischmanns, New York: Purple Mountain Press, 1999.

Potter, Beatrix. *Beatrix Potter's Letters.* Selected by Judy Taylor. London: Frederick Warne, 1989.

Prochnik, George. *Putnam Camp: Sigmund Freud, James Jackson Putnam, and the Purpose of American Psychology.* New York: Other Press, 2006.

Pumpelly, Raphael. *Across America and Asia: Notes of a Five Years' Journey around the World.* New York: Leypoldt & Holt, 1870. Chapter 14, John La Farge, "An Essay on Japanese Art."

Pumpelly, Raphael. *My Reminiscences.* 2 vols. New York: Henry Holt, 1918. There is surprisingly little here on Dublin, even in the chapter on Dublin, II: 656-662, where his house is pictured opposite p. 656.

Reid, Robert Leonard, ed. *A Treasury of the Sierra Nevada.* Berkeley, California: Wilderness Press, 1983.

Rice, Howard C. "Brattleboro in the 1800's and 1890: Cabots, Balestiers and Kiplings," *English Literature in Transition*, 1880-1920, v.29, #2, 1986, 150-160.

Rice Jr., Howard C. "Rudyard Kipling's House in Vermont," *Vermont Life*, Spring 1952, 34-39.

Rice, Howard C. *Rudyard Kipling in New England*. Brattleboro, Vermont: Book Cellar, 1951.

Richardson, Robert D. *William James: In the Maelstrom of American Modernism: A Biography*. Boston: Houghton Mifflin, 2006.

Ricketts, Harry. *Rudyard Kipling: A Life*. New York: Carroll & Graf, 2000.

Rosenzweig, Saul. *Freud, Jung, and Hall the King-maker: The Historic Expedition to America (1909)*. Kirkland, Washington: Hogrefe & Huber Publishers, 1992.

Sargent, Shirley. *Yosemite's Historic Wawona*. Yosemite, California: Flying Spur Press, 1979.

Scott, Frederick J. Down, "William James' 1898 Visit to California," *San Jose Studies*, February 1977, 7-22.

Scott, Frederick J. Down, "William James's 1895 Visit to Colorado," *San Jose Studies*, May 1979, 33-40.

Shaw, Donald E. *Trolley Days in Brattleboro, Vermont*. Springfield, Massachusetts, 27 June 1947. Copy in Brattleboro Historical Society.

Shields, Allan, "William James Visits Yosemite in 1898," *Yosemite Association*, Summer 2001.

Simon, Linda. *Genuine Reality: A Life of William James*. New York: Harcourt Brace, 1998.

Solnit, Rebecca. *Wanderlust: A History of Walking*. New York: Viking Penguin, 2000.

Stewart, D.H., ed. *Kipling's America: Travel Letters, 1889-1895*. Greensboro, North Carolina:: ELT Press, 2003. "In Sight of Monadnock," 202-209. William B. Dillingham's excellent review, *ELT* 47:3 2004, 331-335, relates RK's rebuke of America's optimism and boasting of mostly its material progress.

Swift, Esther Munroe, *Vermont Place-Names*. Camden, Maine: Picton Press, 1977, 1996.

Taliaferro, John. *All the Great Prizes: The Life of John Hay, from Lincoln to Roosevelt*. New York: Simon & Schuster, 2013. 295.

Thoreau, Henry D. *The Maine Woods*. Joseph J. Moldenhauer, ed. Princeton, New Jersey: Princeton University Press, 1972.

Thoreau, Henry D. *Reform Papers*. Wendell Glick, ed. Princeton, New Jersey: Princeton University Press, 1973.

Thoreau, Henry D. "Walking," *Excursions*. Joseph J. Moldenhauer, ed. Princeton, New Jersey: Princeton University Press, 2007.

Thoreau, Henry D. *Walden*. J. Lyndon Shanley, ed. Princeton, New Jersey: Princeton University Press, 1971.

Thorson, Robert M. *Beyond Walden: The Hidden History of America's Kettle Lakes and Ponds* (New York: Walker & Co., 2009), Kettle, 1 (defined), Lake Sunapee, 28. Lake Chocorua, 141, 240.

Tolles, Jr, Bryant F. *Resort Hotels of the Adirondacks: The Architecture of a Summer Paradise, 1850-1950*. Hanover, NH: University Press of New England, 2003.

Tolles, Jr, Bryant F. *Summer Cottages in the White Mountains: The Architecture of Leisure and Recreation, 1870-1930*. Hanover, New Hampshire: University Press of New England, 2000.

Townsend, Kim. *Manhood at Harvard: William James and Others*. New York: W.W. Norton, 1997. Tom Lutz, *NYT Book Review*, 5 January 1997, 16-17. James is "the hero of this book because he best articulated the strenuous ideal and most clearly saw its negative..."

Tweit, Susan J. "A Beautiful Resurrection," *Zone* 4, Summer 2009.

Tweit, Susan J. *Walking Nature Home: A Life's Journey*. Austin, Texas: University of Texas Press, 2009.

The Vermont Difference: Perspectives from the Green Mountain State. Eds: J. Kevin Graffagnino, H. Nicholas Muller III, David A. Donath, Kristin Peterson-Ishaq. Woodstock, Vermont: The Woodstock Foundation/Barre, Vermont: The Vermont Historical Society, 2014.

Waterman, Laura and Guy. *Forest and Crag: A History of Hiking, Trail Blazing, and Adventure in the Northeast Mountains*. Boston: Appalachian Mountain Club, 1989.

Wessels, Tom. *The Granite Landscape: A Natural History of America's Mountain Domes, from Acadia to Yosemite*. Woodstock, Vermont: The Countryman Press, 2001. Black Mt., 12-18; Chocorua; 11-12, 99-101; Whites and Adirondacks,93-110.

Wessels, Tom, "Parables of Place," in *Where the Mountain Stands Alone*, 65-72. Lake Ashuelot. Great September 1815 Gale leveled summit red spruce, which fed fire of early 1820s. Sheep fever, 1810-1840, clears forest for pasture.Wantastiquet's tall white pines and fires.

Where the Mountain Stands Alone: Stories of Place in the Monadnock Region. Howard Mansfield, ed. Lebanon, NH: University Press of New England, 2006. The cover is detail of Alexander James's painting of Monadnock in 1944 (?) from Nancy Hayden's Too Bad Farm, Marlborough, NH. After James's September 1943 heart attack, Hayden's grandmother asked him to paint the view from the farm for the joy of it (356).

Wilkins, Thurman. *Clarence King: A Biography.* 1958. Albuquerque, New Mexico: University of New Mexico Press, 1988.

Wilson, Andrew. *A President's Love Affair with the Lake District.* Windermere, Cumbria: Lakeland Press Agency, 1996.

The Papers of Woodrow Wilson. Arthur S. Link, ed. Volume 18: 1908-1909. Princeton, New Jersey: Princeton University Press, 1974.

Wulf, Andrea. *The Invention of Nature: Alexander von Humboldt's New World.* New York: Alfred A. Knopf, 2015.

INDEX

Goddard, Elizabeth Cass, 36, 41

Goldmark, Pauline, 8, 46, WJ's first meeting, Keene Valley; 72, Hopkins; 75, Marcy. Letters to: 79, 93, 106, 118, 123, 125

Green Mountains, VT, 49, 51-56

Hall, G. Stanley, 125

Hancock, NH, 32,109-113

Harvey, Charles (architect of Hotel Champlain), 73

Hay, John, 22; summer home, Lake Sunapee, NH, 24

Higginson, Henry Lee, Rock Harbor, Westport, NY, 72. Letter to: 98

Hill, Edward (artist), 87, with brother Thomas in White Mountains, NH

Hill, Thomas (artist), 87

Hoevenberg, Henry Van (Manager Adirondack Lodge), 34, 74, outfit; 92, visit

Hooker, George White, 19

Howard, Matthew (Kipling's coachman), 18.

Howison, George Holmes, 8, 88

Hudson, William Henry (naturalist), 9-10

Humboldt, Alexander von, 6, volcanoes of the Andes

Hunt, Jonathan and Jane, 19

Hunt, Richard Morris, birthplace, 19; architect of Biltmore, 103

Hunt William Morris (artist), 19, birthplace; 64, Boston studio

Isserman, Maurice, 4

Jacobs, Harriet, Cambridge innkeeper, 29. 30

James, Alexander (son of WJ; artist), 32

James, Alice (sister of WJ), 28, 31

James, Alice Howe Gibbens (wife of WJ), marriage and honeymoon, 45; 67-68, ascent of Mt Chocorua (1897); 81-82, early life in California; 89, discovery of her father's farm in Mountain View, CA

James, Garth Wilkinson (brother of WJ), 13

James, Henry (father of WJ), 12-13

James, Henry Jr (brother of WJ):
Switzerland (1860), 3-4;
Kipling wedding, 17-18;
"Maud-Evelyn;" 88;
Lamb House, Rye, England, 99, 127;
Letter to HJ, 100;
at Chocorua, 106;
with Edith Wharton in Berkshires (1904),124

James, William: change, 13;
Harvard Medical School, 7;
holidays, 8; benefits of nature, 8; travel, 12, 30-31; writings: "On a Certain Blindness," 8;